MW00623633

Yesterday's Noise

Also by Joe Mackall

MEMOIR

The Last Street Before Cleveland

Plain Secrets: An Outsider Among the Amish

ANTHOLOGY

River Teeth: 20 Years of Creative Nonfiction

Yesterday's Noise

A Family Legacy of Rage and Radiance

Essays

Joe Mackall

The Humble Essayist
Press

The Humble Essayist Press
Blairsville, Georgia

Copyright © 2021 Joe Mackall

All Rights Reserved

ISBN: 1734517727

ISBN-13: 978-1-7345177-2-9

To my four granddaughters, Ellie, Cassie, Madison, and Harper,
with all the love that's in me.

And to the memory of my uncle, Dick Mackall, (1930-2020).
The best there ever was.

*"How sweet the past is, no matter how wrong, or how
Sad.
How sweet is yesterday's noise."*
Charles Wright

TABLE OF CONTENTS

Introduction

On the evening of August 18, 1805, while camped on the Jefferson River in southwestern Montana, Meriwether Lewis, co-captain of the Corps of Discovery, wrote the following in his journal: "This day I completed my thirty-first year. I conceive that I have in all human probability now existed about half the period that I am which to remain in the Sublunary world. I reflected that I had as yet done but little, very little indeed to further the happiness of the human race or to advance the information of the succeeding generation. I viewed with regret the many hours I have spent in indolence, and now soarly (sic) feel the want of that information which those hours would have given me had they been judiciously expended. But since they are past and cannot be recalled, I dash from me the gloomy thought and resolved in future, to redouble my exertions and at least indeavour (sic) to promote those two primary objects of human existence, by giving them the aid of that portion of my talents which nature and fortune have bestowed on me; or in the future, to live for *mankind* as

I have heretofore lived *for myself.*—"

It appears to me that Lewis is being pretty tough on himself. He's only thirty-one after all. After serving as Thomas Jefferson's personal secretary, he's now on a mission to cross the entire United States on an expedition people will celebrate for more than two centuries. He and William Clark had been sent by Jefferson to discover the so-called Northwest Passage, the imagined endless water route from ocean to ocean. Nobody knew then that no such passage existed, but nobody can take away from the success of the expedition when it came to scientific advancement in the areas of flora and fauna, as well as the general knowledge gained about the American West and its indigenous people.

I'm struck by Lewis's sense of obligation to future generations, his life-long struggle with his own dark thoughts, his desire to do more, to live more fully and to live for others. I have always identified with Meriwether Lewis, although I fall far short of his brilliance and his ostensible altruism. I do, however, identify with his deep melancholy, his attachment to the past, and his hopes for the future. My goals, however, are far humbler than those of Captain Lewis.

I turned sixty-two on August 19, 2020, and despite the ways I fail to measure up to Meriwether Lewis in fame or intelligence, I too bemoan how little I have accomplished. Perhaps all people of a certain age begin to look back at their lives in wonder. Why did I do this? Why didn't I do that? Could I have done more? Is there still sufficient time? Some enviable folks no doubt possess the evolutionarily sound ability to ignore the past and look only at the present and the future. I am not one of these. History humbles and haunts me. I have been sustained and nurtured by stories of past generations, some from my country and some from family, many that intersect. I would not say that I am a prisoner of the past, but I am certainly caught up in it—by how today becomes yesterday. The poet Charles Wright speaks to my sensibilities perfectly in these few lines: "It's 1936, in Tennessee. I'm one./ And spraying the dead grass with a hose/ The curtains blow in and out./ And then it's not. And I'm not and they're not."

In my early sixties—an age the novelist William Styron called "the hulking milestone of mortality"—I find myself pinioned between past and future, struggling but mostly failing to abide in the present. It doesn't help that my wife and I live in a small, rural lake community among four generations of my family. My father lives across the lake, and my daughter, her husband and two of my granddaughters also reside on the lake's shores. Days collide with each other in disorienting ways. Although my father is a fit, vigorous and optimistic eighty-nine-year-old man, he speaks often of the life behind him, the folks he's lost, the minor regrets he holds. He has lived his life as a man always planning for the future, which is a philosophy that doesn't offer much to someone nearing ninety. I often enter the past with him in the mornings and by late afternoon my granddaughters are eager to propel me into their moment, the present that's illuminated by the world of the senses, where we allow ants and crickets to crawl up our naked arms, beholding and narrating what we believe to be an epic odyssey. Even as I play or explore the present with my granddaughters, I can't help fearing for their futures. While brushing an ant from my arm, I'll begin wondering what I have inherited from my ancestors. How have their lives affected my life? Did they die secure in the knowledge that they had improved the planet for future generations? (Is that question merely grandiose?) How have I been shaped by their stories? Why are some defined by their tragedies? Some by a marriage? Others by resentments? A few by their work? Too many by violence? What am I offering my own grandchildren? Which stories will they tell of their time with their grandparents? In a deeply personal way, I share Lewis's sense of responsibility to succeeding generations.

I am certainly a flawed parent and grandparent, but also a loving one. I adore my four granddaughters, but I worry about them, their country, their world. I ache wondering what my generation could have done better. Should have made better. My anxiety grows by the day as I consider which forces across the world, among their immediate families, or darkly at work in the universe of cells in their own fledgling bodies, will bear down on their lives. And how much of what does occur will lie beyond my control? Although I manage to remain sanguine a good deal of the time, in my most glum moments, at times even while watching my granddaughters frolic innocently in the sunshine of a beautiful summer morning, I believe utterly in an assertion made by a character in Jess Walter's novel *The Cold Millions*, that "The world was built to eat you alive."

The essays in *Yesterday's Noise* are not an attempt to answer my endless and admittedly gloomy queries, but they are an attempt to explore them. I like to think that with these essays I am embarking on a drastically dwarfed shadow version of the Corps of Discovery.

Lewis would be wrong on how long he had yet to live. Lost in drink and despair, he committed suicide just four years after this journal entry, three years after returning from the Pacific Ocean, too soon after entering history. He never married and sired no offspring. In that I have far outdone him. It is my family, past and present, that sustains me and exhausts me. I understand that love is all we have, and I also realize how vulnerable love makes us. As the writer Terry Tempest Williams writes, "We need to learn how to live and love with a broken heart."

What I'm trying to do in this book, I suppose, is learning how to carry my love and devotion for the past, and my fear and hopes for the future, all the while remaining upright, bending toward beauty.

Grandparents in Paradise: Life in the Face of the Fall

As the day nears dusk, I watch as my oldest granddaughter runs out of our house toward a car full of other high school kids. The girl behind the wheel—somewhere between sixteen and the rest of her life—is a little overweight, which for some reason comforts me, until I notice she wears the too thick makeup of a young woman wanting a life she doesn't yet understand. A boy jumps out of the rustbelt Buick to let Ellie in the backseat. I don't like the kid right off; I know he can't be trusted. His movements are too deliberate. He acts as if perpetually aware of a camera. He has too beautiful hair. He doesn't even acknowledge my wife or me as we smile miserably from the front porch. I hear the tinkling of an empty can spilling out of the car and hitting our driveway. Assuming it's a Miller or Bud, I tense; my muscles clench. I then feel the warmth of my wife's fingers on my arm, which is just enough to keep me still. Ellie tosses us a casual wave over her shoulder and disappears into the Buick, into the world. The world outside of our family and our home has been whispering to her since she was old enough to realize there was something else out there. It beckons

us all, of course. But on this day, it echoes with the wail of pain.

But I'm just imagining this. Ellie's only four years old. She still has her favorite blanket she calls her "night night." She never runs out of our house unless it's to play in our yard. As a matter of fact, she hates leaving our home, even to go back to her own, to parents she loves and who love her. But I know this will change. It has to. It's the way of the world, which, to me, is little consolation. I recall being eager for my own three children to grow up, accrue resources for living, become independent. When it comes to my granddaughters, however, I'm often paralyzed with fear at the thought of their entering the wider world. And I'm not exactly sure why.

I admit I've been blindsided by becoming a grandfather. Before we had grandkids, I'd professed my vision of our life to come. I told my wife, Dandi, that we'd buy the kids anything they needed, take them on vacations, pay for college, leave them money, make sure they had the best life and most boundless love we could give them, but I did not want to be involved in the day to day. I did not see myself as a babysitter or as a second layer of parent. I did not want my life defined by becoming a grandfather. My desire was to drift in the sweet stratosphere of benign neglect. Dandi has promised to waterboard me if I ever express a desire to walk around a mall wearing a "World's Greatest Grandpa" t-shirt.

Now I can't go more than three or four days without aching to see the girls. My whole way of being wavers in their presence. My dark disposition begins to lighten up; at least it does when they're around. I figured out some of it. After a quarter century of loving all the same people, I've fallen in love with somebody new. I've loved my children all of their lives and my wife every day for nearly twenty-five years, but now there's new love. Perhaps my heart's tectonic shifts have shaken my psychic geography. I have two new people to love, two new people to see the world through, to share life with, to worry about, to fear for in a time when I sometimes can't recognize my own country and when the world's people appear easily connected electronically and so dangerously disconnected in just about every other conceivable way.

I often feel as though I'm moving toward the edge of a foreign land, the plains of an emotional dystopia. I know it's connected in ways I don't fully understand to life as a grandfather and as a man in his fifties, life as an American in a country increasingly polarized, fracked, outsourced, droned, downsized, teetering on the dream-edge of itself. As a writer, editor, a full, tenured professor, I have work I love and am still young and coherent enough to do. I also know what's out there waiting for me: impotence, probably; incontinence, likely; dementia, some adverb I can't come up with right now; senior moments, and then, surely, no moments at all. I have a great family, a wife I cherish, loving children, and two wondrous granddaughters. My father's alive and well and lives a couple miles from me. My granddaughters too live only minutes away. My son is healthy and happy and married to a young woman I adore. And just beyond all this peace and love I perceive the vague existence of foreboding or surrender or something I've not allowed myself to imagine. I'm gazing through paradise and seeing into the shadow of the fall.

My oldest granddaughter, Ellie, lives awash in awe and wonder, and she's even splashed some of it onto my penchant for lazy cynicism and dark moods. When it rains, she wants to run outside and hold it as it falls. "Let's go catch the rain, Pa." That's who I am to her: Pa. "The stars are like candles in the sky, Pa." When my daughter asked what I'd like the kids to call me, I was ready with a name: Santiago. Granted it would have been tough for a toddler to say, but I figured one could learn in time. It beat the hell out of being called "bappo" or "fafa" or "gragra" or some other hideous title. I gave up on Santiago, however, when I imagined the girls referring to me as "Sans" until they could say Santiago. It would be as though my name to them were "without." As in sans serif. I just couldn't live being without. I like the sound of Pa; it's solid, permanent. Pa's what the boy called his dad *The Rifleman* on the eponymous show. And also how Ben's *Bonanza* boys addressed him. Pa sounds like the frontier; it pushes through the small universe of our home with the gravitas of time and history, even if only pop culture history.

I used to love July 2 for literary reasons, and I would take the day off no matter where I was employed, volunteering to work on the Fourth for anybody who wanted to trade with me. I honored this day because it was the date of Hemingway's death. Now it's my holiday because on July 2, a month before she turned two, Ellie said, as casual as you please when I walked into the room, "Hi, Pa," for the first time.

I also revere the day Ellie learned to say the word *No*. I laugh the celebratory laugh of the mad whenever Ellie says it. "No, Pa. No, Momma. No bath. No, Dadda. No home. No carrots. No. No. No." And the louder and more aggressively she says it, the louder I laugh and the more I celebrate. All young girls ought to scream the word No—early and often.

Every time Ellie's over she rings a small bell by our open kitchen window to summon birds to their feeder. And sometimes, as if she's been transformed into a diminutive disciple of St. Francis, they fly to her. I so succumb to her view of the world at moments like this that it's hard for me to imagine that not every bird on every tree in a thousand-mile radius doesn't hasten to the music of her bell. This is part of what frightens me. She has weakened my foundation. If I'm cynical and skeptical and given to pessimism and the unforgiving but familiar company of the black dog, I'm psychically safe, at least that's the myth I've lived by. Don't leave yourself too vulnerable to things like hope and optimism and faith. Like Robert Duvall's character in the film *Tender Mercies*, "You see, I don't trust happiness. Never did and I never will." Perhaps Ellie's wonder is nothing more than the lingua franca of innocence and it's something unavailable, or even unhealthy, for a middle-aged man. I then console myself with Robert Penn Warren's admonition that when one becomes an adult, "…it is too late to pretend we are children at dusk watching fireflies."

Perhaps the most frightening development of becoming a grandfather is that I no longer trust time. I'm as spastic in time as Billy Pilgrim. When my oldest daughter was in the hospital having our second granddaughter, Cassie, Ellie stayed at our house for thirty-six hours or so. When we dropped her off, I wept, sobbed even, for reasons I didn't understand. My wife looked at me, wary. She knows I'm prone to clinical depression and often, even when I'm feeling good, take melancholy as a lover, at least for an afternoon, or during a soft rain, or the nights after heart-soaked holidays. But on this day, she really didn't understand. And that made two of us.

Sure, I was tired—Ellie eschews sleep and likes to play all night when she stays at our house—but it was more than that. Sure, I was emotionally vulnerable because my daughter had just given birth to another little girl. Sure, these had to be tears of joy. But I knew better. Even while crying, thoughts of my son, then twenty-seven, bubbled up from my subconscious, thoughts of all those weekends after his mother, my first wife, and I divorced. All those grim Sunday nights I dropped him at home, his real home, from the time he was two until he entered college. I'd be in nearly equal parts anguished he didn't live with me, guilty his parents couldn't stay married, relieved my diligent weekend duties were over, guilty again for that, but mainly sad that things were as broken as they were. And somehow all of that came back to me when my wife and I took Ellie back to her parent's house, not ten minutes away from our own.

My granddaughters have accomplished something believed only by certain physicists, science fiction writers and fantasists. They've made time travel possible. I'm living in a new world where the past, present and future cohere and exist simultaneously. Ellie could be sitting in her highchair with Dandi and me at her side, the three of us exultant, laughing and singing, when I'm believing in the possibility of our living room windows bursting from the sheer force of compressed joy; and in that same moment, I'll suddenly experience a paroxysm of deep regret over something I did or did not do with my own children, or of leaving my son alone with his mother. I'm suddenly hovering over the moment, levitated by grief and longing, imagining the two of them laughing; my son then looking over to where I should be standing. Sans dad. And in the next instant I'll wonder how long we'll all have each other. Will Dandi undergo another surgery or experience a second heart attack? Will we be around when Ellie's fifteen or twenty or married or a mother or a nuclear physicist? And by the time I alight back on the present, the moment I'd inhabited will be gone forever. I'm sure it doesn't help that we live in an era when the Internet seems to have flattened the globe and erased some of time's boundaries. It also doesn't help that I'm neurotic as hell. I struggle to stay tethered to the present, which is, according to C.S. Lewis, when we're the nearest to eternity.

Perhaps I need to become more like my father, who does not define himself by father, grandfather or great-grandfather. Although a loving man and a wonderful dad and granddad, he's clearly lived on his own terms. While he adores his twenty-eight grandkids, he's perfectly fine letting his life remain separate from theirs. Perhaps it's the sheer number of grandchildren he has, but I suspect it has more to do with his character. There are those who act and those who worry and wonder. He also has five great-grandchildren, and when I recently asked him the name of the newest, he couldn't recall the baby's gender. The father of a good friend of mine, a Swartzentruber Amish man, has over one hundred grandchildren. He once told me that if he sat down with a couple of his kids and a pencil and paper, he might be able to come up with most of their names.

I realize my reaction to becoming a grandfather is not typical, perhaps not even normal. Let me assure you, it gets worse. A few confessions: I resisted getting new carpet in our library because Ellie and Cassie had crawled upon the old. I've let Ellie cover every inch of my bald pate with Strawberry Shortcake stickers. I mourned the day she stopped watching the *Wonder Pets*. I still miss Linny, Tuck and Ming-Ming, too. I've tucked a small blanket into my belt and, having been transformed into a princess by Ellie, danced around our living room, spinning until dizzy, my blanket billowing around me like a jeweled ball gown on a hippo prancing and pretty in a field of poppy.

I want to begin saying No to the girls, but I don't trust myself. I fear that if I start, I'll never stop. I'm afraid I'll say things like: Don't catch the acid rain. Don't say hello to everybody you see. Don't open your heart too wide. Don't see the stars as candles in the sky. Don't feel so much. Don't see so much beauty. Don't count on anybody to be your prince or princess. Not even Pa. Somewhere along the line, your heart will break and mine will follow. At the same time, I want them to embrace imagination so that, to paraphrase Wallace Stevens, the imagination can push back against the pressure of reality and help them live their lives.

I experienced none of this with my own children. Perhaps I was just too busy working and worrying about economic and marital survival to imagine time ever passing in a way that confounded me. I know I've become more neurotic and sentimental since being a young father, but that doesn't explain everything.

I want my granddaughters to "skate upon the intense radiance" of life's miracles, as John Updike once wrote in an e-mail, as he strove to catch his breath, having just come in from playing in the yard with his grandchildren. But I also want them, when the time's right, to scream the scream of No.

And this is what I mean, in part, about seeing through paradise and living in the face of the fall. Our kids are in their twenties. Our granddaughters are toddlers. Our careers are healthy. We aren't yet old. I realize that because of a recent operation and heart attack, my wife has been sick, and our family life split into a before and after. I've known forever that our youngest daughter has a debilitating and progressive kidney disease, along with severe neurological problems, and that she's nearly blind and deaf, and that her life and longevity have surprised her doctors more than once. I know my wife fears not being around to watch her granddaughters grow up. I know that we're both, maybe we're all, uncertain of the America our country's becoming. I know all of this as surely as I know I'm living in paradise, living in the face of the fall. I'm alive in a paradise of rage and radiance, a land engulfed in love and in the knowledge that love may not be enough, a paradise of fear and the wonder of hope, as we age each new dawn and children dive into cars and drive deep into the night.

Stop-time #1

"Recent analyses of fossil teeth indicate that grandparents were rare in ancient populations, such as those of the australopithecines and the Neandertals. [Grandparents] first became common around 30,000 years ago, as evidenced by remains of early modern Europeans." (*Scientific American*)

The Little Girl at the Door

The doorbell rings and I know before I answer it who will be standing on our misnamed welcome mat. It will be the intruder. A threat to my family. A domestic terrorist. An eight-year-old child.

Sure enough it's the girl from the next street asking if my granddaughter is visiting. The little shit seems to have a sixth sense about Ellie's visits. What I hate admitting to myself or anybody else is that I fear this child. The house she lives in screams of too much activity and not enough care. Too many people come and go. The little girl's older brother walks down our street in shorts and without shoes to catch the school bus in the middle of an Ohio winter. He's either deranged or his parents don't give a damn. Seven years ago I would have worried about the boy getting sick, wondering if he was receiving the love and care he deserved, agonizing over what misery drove him barefoot and broken into a February morning. But that was seven years ago. In certain important ways, I'm much less of a person now.

I hear the knock again. My wife answers the door. She tells the child that Ellie would *love* to come out and play. Her greeting sounds annoyingly cheerful and welcoming. Ellie, six years old next month, seems to like the little girl, but Ellie likes everybody. My wife accompanies her outside, but I stay in the house. I don't like sharing my granddaughters with anybody, but my anxiety about this girl goes deeper than that.

I look out the window and watch Ellie and the little girl at the door run around in front of our house. All I hear is what one would expect to hear: little girls laughing, their sharp, small exchanges piercing a placid summer evening, their shrill voices like tiny tears in a leaf.

I imagine the little girl and Ellie walking around the neighborhood in a few years, acting bored, smoking cigarettes, being pursued by boys I know all too well, romantic young boys lured by the hum of dusk, boys bruised by a world they don't understand, boys eager to bruise back.

I was far more empathetic right before and immediately after my granddaughters were born. For their first couple of years on earth I even entertained delusions of becoming a better human being. I was moved anew by the world and its wonders, at times joyful to the point of idiocy. But then something changed. I woke up one morning realizing that I could no longer afford not to judge people, especially people like the family of the little girl at the door. A family, I should add, I do not know and have never met. The house is unkempt and neglected. The whole place reminds me more than a little of where I grew up. Small ranch houses filled with factory workers and their families. Houses and lawns unseen to by parents who worked fourteen-hour days to feed the children the Catholic Church encouraged them to rhythmically deliver into the world.

I continue watching two little girls run around our front yard. I want nothing more in life at this moment than for this child to leave our home. I don't want her to return, not ever. I don't want to care for her. I don't want to worry about her. I don't want to wake up in the middle of the night considering what I may owe her. I don't want to be the sensitive progressive I believe myself to be. We can't save everybody.

Not a word of this comes out of my mouth. I don't want to witness my wife's knees buckle in shame. I don't want her to look at me with eyes that wonder who the hell it is she's been married to all these years. I turn from her gaze, holding tight my anger and fear, but mostly my shame, watching my granddaughter and the little girl at the door run smiling through dappled grass.

As she's leaving, the little girl picks up her bike and skillfully spins it, aiming her front tire toward the street. I'm awed by the artfulness of her move. She tosses her head back, smiles, waves, pedals away. I watch her through my reflection in the window, and I see us both clearly—someone to love, someone to fear.

Stop-time #2

Near the end of his life, Teddy Roosevelt, after suffering immense personal loss, including the death of his father when the future president was just a boy, followed by the death of his mother and his first wife in the same house on the same day, and finally by losing his son in World War I, "[he] had made up his mind," a family member wrote, "that he would have to suffer for some time to come. And with high courage had adjusted himself to bear it. Since Quentin was killed he has been sad. Only Ethel's little girl—[Roosevelt's baby granddaughter]—had the power to make him merry.

A Death in the Family

Decades after fleeing New York in the middle of the night as Al Capone and his men sought revenge for hijacked booze, my maternal grandfather, Cosimo Leo Gervasi (Leo to his wife of seventy-two years), elbows his twelve-year-old grandson as they sit in St. James Catholic Church one hot, summer Sunday.

I look to him and he's laughing and pointing. I see where he's pointing and witness a fly landing on the gigantic backside of a devout woman in a blue dress. The fly lands and lifts off, lands again and lifts off as if it has found an alternate universe. Leo laughs and points, laughs and points. It's clear to me even then that this is one of those moments; one I'll remember for its quiet knowing and its singular joy. An old man and a young boy bored at church, reaching out through generations, grateful for a funny and irreverent moment. I also see it as a shared moment with an icon, a great character in an archetypal American story.

At that moment I was happy for the shared laugh and the distraction from the service. Also, my maternal grandfather was not a man who joked easily or often. Although he'd always treated me well and I felt confident that he loved me and his other fifteen grandchildren, I'd grown up hearing stories of his stern disposition and strident anger. Even though he stood no taller than five six and weighed not an ounce over 140 pounds, his three sons feared him. It's not going too far to say they at times hated him, never getting from him what they needed. He was not a man to tell his sons he loved them, so he never did. As much as they needed it said, they never heard the words from his lips, not once. He lived to be ninety-two. His four daughters adored him, as did his grandchildren no matter their gender.

He took great pride in his small rose garden, and I remember him walking me through it, pointing out the color, size and beauty, taking pride in the petals and thorns he'd wrought from the earth. As I write this, I wonder if he treated me so well because I was the oldest son of his youngest daughter, a daughter who'd survived a sickly childhood. My aunts and uncles always marveled that my mother survived as long as she did, and how lucky we all were that she had. Leo and his wife, Anna, my grandmother, had already buried one daughter. Baby Eva, as she'd be known for decades after her death, had died after only a year of life. She died the same day another daughter had come down with pneumonia, the same day Leo lost his job during the Depression.

How long the fly frolicked on the devout woman's duvet-sized backside I cannot recall. I do know that in the miasma of memory it frolics still, conjuring a man I called Gramps, a man who sailed to America at age twelve expecting to join an uncle who'd be waiting for him on the shores of a new world. While on board, Leo used a hunk of cheese given to him by his mother as a pillow. Unbeknownst to young Leo, that uncle had left New York City and was en route back to southern Italy. Leo landed on Ellis Island, alone, never to see his family again, not knowing a word of English, not knowing another human being.

He gravitated toward the thousands of other Italians newly arrived in New York City in the early years of a new century. One of his early jobs was cleaning spittoons. He soon got to know a young boy named Frankie Uale, Americanized as Yale, who would become his best friend. Two decades after arriving in New York City, Leo would flee the city in the middle of a late winter night, never telling his wife or children where he was going, only that he'd get in touch once it was safe. Leo found safe haven in Cleveland, where, five decades later, he'd nudge his young grandson's elbow to share a laugh about a fly on a fat woman. The reason Leo fled New York remained a secret for years.

Cosimo Leo Gervasi has been dead for nearly forty years. I still regret not being present for his interment. Newly married and miserable at a job I hated in Lexington, Kentucky, I was allowed to go to Cleveland for only a day. I wish now I'd had the guts to tell my employers that I'd need more time, that I believed the earth should stand still for this man's death, at least for a few days, that he'd done great things, that he'd lived a life that demanded notice, that I needed to be in Cleveland more than they needed me to sauté their meals and manage their then-trendy crepe restaurant. I hated the job, but I had a young wife and a one-year-old son. I needed the money. I needed the stability. So the three of us drove to Cleveland, went to the funeral home viewing, and then drove back to Kentucky, sixteen hours total. Not nearly enough time to bury a legend.

The Private Wars of a Dying Storyteller

As I watch my grandmother sleep, disturbing images of Al Capone and Frankie Yale descend on our visit. Checking to make sure the oxygen tubes are securely in her nose, I can almost see Yale driving his black sedan that July day of 1927, the day he earned the dubious distinction of being the first New York gangster killed by a tommy gun.

Yale, nicknamed the Executioner, had been supervising the Long Island shin of Capone's bootleg business, while Scarface ran the Chicago operation. Yale began hijacking the booze and keeping the money, or Capone just thought that was going on, which in those days with those men amounted to the same thing. Whatever the case, on Sunday, July 1, Yale died in a flurry of Capone-ordered bullets.

But my grandmother and history differ in their stories of Yale. Because Yale took an ocean-orphaned Italian immigrant under his tainted wing, my grandmother considered him an ally in her war with a new century, a new country. She knew nothing of Yale's reputation or his business; she understood only that he helped a twelve-year-old Italian immigrant boy who was to become her husband.

My grandmother wakes from her sleep, pats me on the hand and asks how my wife is, how my children are. "How old are they now?" she asks. I selfishly want her to stay awake long enough to tell me stories, stories about the "old neighborhood," but before I can ask a leading question, she is back to sleep. I check the oxygen tubes to make sure she is getting what she needs.

I do not need to hear stories about Yale; a story about anybody from the old neighborhood will do. When I was a kid, I believed that my aunts and uncles lived the most extraordinary lives anyone has ever lived. My beliefs were not based on the facts of their lives, but rather the stories. My grandmother had the ability to transmute her children and their friends into memorable characters in the drama called the "Old Neighborhood."

One such character is Tommy Tanzio. Tommy's mother died the day of her son's eighth birthday. After that, my uncle, then thirteen, walked Tommy to school every day on orders from my grandmother. The walk to St. Thomas Aquinas had one detour, which was a bar, where Tommy's father supposedly would be, drunk, usually asleep. Tommy would walk over to his father, kiss him on the forehead and take a quarter out of his pocket. No matter how drunk Mr. Tanzio had been the night before or how much money he had spent, there would always be a quarter waiting for Tommy. From the bar to the school the two boys raced. Tommy always won.

My grandmother wakes up long enough to ask me to wet her lips, which are so dry they're cracked. As I do it, her tongue moves in and out of her mouth, as if preparing to launch us on a voyage of story. Instead, she again asks me the ages of my children. Again I tell her.

She also had a World War II repertoire, which concentrated not on the horrors or heroics of the battlefield but rather the nuances of the home front. One of my uncles spent the war in the belly of a gunner. Not until years after the war was he able to surrender the booze, and his transformation into an upstanding citizen has something to do with a Christmas tree falling on him early one Christmas morning or late one Christmas Eve. I learned something important about storytelling from the Christmas tree tale: Sometimes bits and pieces become the whole.

On V-E Day, women and their daughters, old men and young boys took to the streets of Cleveland, banging pots and pans in a raucous, domestic parade of thanks. I'm told the clanging could be heard for hours and for miles.

The day her oldest son returned from overseas, an odd breeze cut through Cleveland. As if confused by natural weather patterns, the wind dipped and dove, blowing first one way, then another, spinning newspapers aloft and then hurtling them flat against fences, only to let them drop to the ground. It is said that it rained on only one side of the street. A knock came at the door. "Do you have any food for a hungry soldier?" As mother and son hugged, the soldier's boots shuffled on the wooden porch on the day the wind seemed possessed.

I heard this story for the first time the week of my tenth birthday, the week I decided that I hated war and loved wooden porches. Now I have a wooden porch. Now I have a son.

At times this noble storyteller still speaks of my grandfather, who has been dead for nearly a decade. He did not tell many stories. He had a heavy and dense Italian accent, and at the age of 70, he had his cancerous larynx removed. My grandmother's hearing is horrible, and to watch these people converse was like watching two angry mimes, desperately in love. Because they were married for more than seventy years, his silence became part of her lore, and her voice part of mine. A narrative oxygen.

My grandmother turns in her sleep, and as she does, I wonder how many untold stories she will be taking with her. How many nuances of being alive in the early part of the 20th Century will I never hear? How much of America dies with each of its elderly?

At a recent family wedding, which my grandmother was too ill to attend, rumors of her deteriorating health and her uncertain future abounded. While family members had historically gravitated to her presence, they seemed to withdraw from her absence.

I remember the last story my grandmother told me. At Christmastime two years ago, my brother and I went to visit her at her house, bringing flowers and groceries, partly out of wanting to bestow her with gifts, partly because we did not visit her often enough. The smell of coffee brewed a five o'clock that morning permeated the air, filling the house with a familial warmth. A small Band-Aid covered a missing chip of paint on the stove.

She began telling a story about something several of her great-grandchildren had done recently. And then, right in the middle of that story, mingled naturally with the children she spoke of, she talked of how while her great-grandchildren played in the yard, they were joined by her youngest child, our mother. My brother and I looked at each other, smiled and looked away. The furnace kicked on, embracing us in an abrupt warmth.

Our mother had been dead for more than twelve years at that time. She never met these particular great-grandchildren; in fact, she died long before they were born. But for my grandmother, her daughter danced and played under the pine tree in the front yard with children from another time.

For that moment, I believe she obtained the perfect mix of storytelling: memory, imagination and desire. Perhaps all of her stories contained this particular mix. Perhaps Tommy went to the bar but found only empty pockets. Maybe the pots and pans weren't all that loud and didn't last quite that long. Perhaps it rained on both sides of the street, and Yale was nothing more than the Executioner.

Some might say that this passing down of stories from one generation to the next can become a perverse and even dangerous romanticism. But what I believe my grandmother passed on is really the hope that things could have been this way, could be this way. Maybe these stories, the beautiful and the dangerous, teach that it is a matter of vision.

Within the next few months, this grand storyteller will probably be moved to a nursing home. How many other of America's forgotten and uncelebrated raconteurs will she join, who tell tales only in the silence of their dreams or as muttered, indiscernible sounds, escaping convenient, drug-induced sleep? I hate to consider it.

I kiss my grandmother on the forehead and tell her I'll visit again soon.

She apologizes for sleeping. She does not realize how much she has given me, nor does she seem to care how little I have given back.

When I step out on the porch, I imagine my mother and my children running beneath the pine, twirling around its trunk until they grow dizzy with the energy and promise of a childhood summer. I smile, nod my head to an unasked question and drive home to my children, wondering which tales I will choose to tell them about their father's visit with the dying storyteller.

The Stories of the Working-Class Lights

We walked along the banks of the creek we called a river, Mole River. Rick and I knew what we had to do. We'd planned the hunt all summer, and the dreaded back to school signs accosted us everywhere we turned. With our new bows strung over our shoulders and arrows tucked in the loops of our jeans, my best friend and I stalked the fields surrounding our blue-collar street, fields shrinking with the arrival of department stores and industrial parkways, fields vanishing as quickly as our childhood summers.

Without success we'd shot at sea gulls that haunted an abandoned drive-in and missed pigeons that polluted the streets. We had the ammunition; we had the urge. Something had to die.

Rick and I reached Mole River by ten in the morning, a trip we thought would take us until at least noon. For our base camp we picked a willow tree whose wispy branches stretched limply over the water, shadowy, skinny fingers reaching out to Mole River. We placed our bagged lunches against the willow's trunk in innocent imitation of our fathers' working-class routines. We, after all, had a job to do. I remember thinking that our sandwiches and cans of pop would stay cool and fresh if nestled in the willow's shade.

I don't recall how many moles died that day, although I do know that I killed only one. I stepped on its tail. The mole jerked back and forth, frantic to escape, its body reduced to a futile pendulum of flesh. I fired. Missed. Fired again. Missed. Thought about the possibility of accidentally running an arrow through my foot. Again, I pulled back the bow and released the arrow. This time a kill. I lifted the mole impaled on the tip of my arrow the way kids roast marshmallows over a campfire.

What else happened that day, I honestly don't know. I'd like to say that Rick and I ate our lunches in silence in the shade of the willow while we considered life and death or the gratuitous murder of our morning. But I can't. I can't because I don't remember. The rest of the day has fallen into the river of time and decomposed. What's left are Rick, a couple of weapons, a willow tree, a living mole, a dead mole, two characters, a story.

For that's what we were that day: characters. And by the time I went mole hunting for the first time, I understood in a way I couldn't yet articulate that the people in my working-class neighborhood would teach me more about storytelling than anyone outside of a book ever could. The storytellers and the characters of my formative years were men who pushed steel in the Chevy plant, the women who packed their lunches—some of whom also pushed steel at Chevy— and the kids who called the steel pushers parents.

It was about the time of the mole hunt that I saw the green light for the first time as it shone in the darkness from a place I could only imagine, a place I suspected but didn't really want to identify.

Although I didn't know it then, the "writers" of my childhood, the men and women who inspired me to dream of becoming a writer, held a pen only to endorse a check or sign a child's report card. It seemed that no matter where I went as a child, stories were as common as the people who told them.

All of my cousins—particularly, male cousins—measured themselves, as I did, against the story of my grandfather leaving kith and kin and sailing from Italy to the United States as a twelve-year-old. A twelve-year-old alone and dreaming. I wished I would have asked my grandfather what he saw in the green light held by the green lady on Liberty Island.

This same grandfather, Cosimo Leo Gervasi, drove a milk truck for years. I grew up hearing stories about how he would let poor families drink milk now and pay for it later. Not only did this story establish my grandfather as a caring and generous man in my young mind, but it also revealed a world where people like our family, people without much money, had to stick together or we wouldn't make it.

On one memorable morning, my grandfather dragged one of his three boys out of bed before dawn to help him on the milk truck. Because in warm weather Cosimo drove his truck with the side doors open and because one of my uncles had been driving the truck that day, a sharp turn hurtled my grandfather out of the truck and into the street. Nobody talked about my grandfather's reaction, but we could all imagine it. All the grandchildren laughed at this story, as did my aunts. My uncles did not. To them it was another story of a too-hard father, a man who pushed his sons ruthlessly and showed them his love not at all.

Shortly before my grandfather would have been eligible for a pension, his milk company "let him go." After years of service, pre-dawn rides and listening to the working-class music of milk bottles rattling metal cages, Cosimo Leo Gervasi was on his own. The moral of this story, according to every member of my extended family, was that "big business" did not care about the little guy. A long line of liberal Democrats emerged.

I believe members of my extended family told these stories because they had to. And I needed to hear them, just as I now need to tell them. I pass them on as I have passed on my DNA. I do not want the line to end. There's too much to lose. I do not want my grandfather forgotten. I do not want the compassionate milkman and the poor family to fall into the silence. I want to remember the morning a father flew out the side of his milk truck. I want to see the red brake lights shining suddenly in the still-cool darkness of early morning. An angry man picking specks of gravel out of his palm. I need to know I came from these stories, these people.

I know this: Sometimes telling the blue-collar stories of generations feels like a kind of loving. Stories are the headlines of the working people. As Leslie Marmom Silko writes, "Stories aren't just entertainment. Don't be fooled. They are all we have, you see, all we have to fight off illness and death. You don't have anything, if you don't have the stories."

My grandmother's house acted as a kind of storytelling central, our family's collective campfire. Stories told in her house seemed to be told in one of two places, either around the dining room table or seated at the kitchen table, and each table seemed to produce a different kind of story. At the spotless, metal kitchen table, my grandmother sat at the head. She would begin by bringing her visitors up to date on all members of the family who were not at the table. I listened to tales of a child's ballet lesson, a toddler's first steps, a cousin's new job. Soon there were stories about an uncle's divorce, a lost job, a teenager in trouble. Because my grandmother had sixteen grandchildren when she died, the stories increased in number as the family increased in size. Soon great-grandchildren became characters in her family stories. Despite all of her storytelling, my grandmother's only writing took place at five in the morning beneath a painting of Jesus praying in Gethsemane, hunched over a rickety wooden desk where she wrote hundreds of Christmas cards.

Surprisingly, girlfriends, boyfriends, and then even husbands and wives not originally part of the family, heard this family folklore not as stories, but rather as banal and boring esoteric gossip. But I knew better. When I heard stories about an elder male cousin earning a 4.0 G.P.A. at a private Jesuit high school, I immediately began measuring myself and my accomplishments against his. This was no mere esoteric gossip; this was a burgeoning family myth. I feared becoming a minor character in a family saga.

My namesake, Uncle Joe, spent his storytelling time at the table weaving tales of the past; he was one of my favorite storytellers. He knew enough about the art of storytelling to tell me tales about my youth, which were important not only because of their subject but also because of the teller's perspective.

"Jumping Joe," he'd say, rubbing his chin pendulum-like across his chest in a nervous gesture or a performer's routine. "You were always jumping up and down in your crib and your PLAYPEN. One day you jumped right OUT." On the final word of every sentence (depending on the story) his voice would seem to leap loudly out of his mouth in a kind of oral high jump.

Uncle Joe also told other tales, but these he told mostly from the dining room table, a huge, old oak table behind which hung a table-size painting of the Last Supper, a painting that inspired greed in the years ahead. He told one story about his time as a soldier in World War II. Somewhere in Europe (I cannot believe I never asked where; I was always too anxious to get to the small story's huge climax.), Uncle Joe came upon the body of a dead German soldier. My uncle found a letter in the soldier's uniform pocket. Somebody in my uncle's platoon could read German and read the letter to the other troops. According to my uncle, the dead soldier had written a letter home to his wife and kids, telling them he loved them, revealing how much he longed to be home, confiding to them that sometimes he didn't know what all the fighting was about.

Uncle Joe took the letter, and had it mailed to his dead enemy's family.

When we were at the dining room table, it usually meant the entire family had gathered for a celebration of some kind. My grandfather's birthday. My grandparents' anniversary. Around the dining room table, the stories always put the family in a larger context. Here I listened to stories of the old neighborhood. When I heard stories about the people from the old neighborhood, people who existed only as characters for me, I began sizing up my own friends and their value as characters in future stories told to as yet unborn children sitting around as yet unbuilt tables. (Even while the mole twitched beneath my boot, I imagined myself preparing to tell that story.) We listened to literal war stories. We heard stories about earlier times in difficult marriages. We heard about the time my uncle Jim ran away from Cleveland at the age of fifteen, and how my grandfather tracked him down in a pool hall in New York City. I have often wondered if this was my uncle's naïve and bungled teenaged attempt to live up to his father's story of emigration and independence.

On the last family reunion, I remember (aside from funerals) my cousins and I reintroduced alcohol to our gatherings. Alcohol appeared to leave our family parties after one year when several of my uncles vomited in the back yard and one of them tried to hide the detritus of their debauchery by covering it with a blanket. It was at least a decade after the beginning of this family-agreed upon prohibition that drinking resurfaced. It seemed like we needed it then. Too much had gone down: an uncle's murder, my grandfather's death, my mother's death, a cousin's fatal car accident, divorces. That night it all seemed to be forgotten. Nearly thirty of us sat around the table, laughing and joking, until somebody successfully coaxed my grandmother into singing "The White Cliffs of Dover," as Christmas-week snow fell past the dining room window. The room fell into the sounds of my grandmother's frail and wounded voice singing a song of war and hope. Soon her juiced up family joined her, believing, I imagine, that she was singing our song.

Recently I visited the street on which I lived from the time I was four until I graduated from college, one field over from where I killed the mole. As I drove, I half expected to see the "old neighborhood" just as I had left it. But what I was probably feeling was a common nostalgia to relive my childhood, to play football until I feared frostbite, to "call" for Mick, Jeff, Rick, and see if we couldn't get a baseball game going in the armory at the end of our street, to visit the homes of the men who worked the line at the Chevy plant, to perhaps catch a glimpse of the boy who wanted to write the stories he was always being told.

I grew up in a world filled with Catholics, a parish of working men and mothering women. There were parish picnics, parties, baseball teams, and Friday fish dinners. Nuns were virgins clad in black habits, and priests were collared mini gods. What amazes me now is how large these families were. Parents with ten or twelve children were forced to clothe their kids in hand-me-down jeans and sweatshirts as they lived from paycheck to paycheck with a ban on birth control and a demand for Catholic school tuition.

Some of these parents—along with thousands of other working-class parents—watched as their sons were sent to Vietnam. Several houses down from the house where I grew up lived a family whose son, Hank, was in Nam. Hank's younger brother, Mike, joined us for football and baseball games, but he never talked about his brother or the war, nor do I remember any of us asking Mike about him, or it. Mike played sports as if he were fighting a war. Tackling him in football hurt the tackler far more than the tacklee. He ran with his knees high and arms flying. He felt hard and looked hard. His black hair hung in greasy strands on his face, looking like a wet, ripped stocking. He had a face prepared for anything, constantly on alert. His sharp nose could pass for a weapon. Unlike the rest of the neighborhood guys, he never invited us into his house. Hank's mother kept a star in the window. Her son came home.

Late one summer night we crept into the armory and spent the night in the back of an army truck. Only three of us survived the night without having to leave in fear; those who retreated were no doubt taunted with invectives, aspersions on their manhood. Most of the night the survivors told stories about waking up in Vietnam ready to fight, kill, die. I slept like a baby. I acted like a fraud. I knew where I stood on the thought of going to war. The Vietnam War moved with its own unending momentum. My father, a Korean War veteran, assured me he would personally drive me to the Canadian border if I were drafted. I loved him for this, and yet I did not completely understand his willingness to make a draft dodger out of his oldest son. Now I have children. Now I understand.

Nearing the end of what was once my street with the Chevy plant looming ahead of me just in front of the setting sun, I almost thought I heard a whistle, my father's whistle, a familial frequency heard across the back lawns and in the benign woods of my neighborhood, a whistle meant for nobody but me, yet understood by neighbors as a beacon of my boyhood. When I'd hear the whistle, I'd bid goodbye to afternoon friends, sprint through the yards and over the lawns of the Smiths, Fays and Murphys; and then, panting, I'd enter the linoleum light and warm smells of a just-dusk kitchen, where a mother now dead and a man who sang by blowing air through his lips would be waiting for me with love as certain as sound.

And yet, despite the fond memories of good friends and love-certain whistles, I grew up feeling the sense of something lost, as if as a member of another generation of working-class kids I would be on the silent side of the secret people like me would never know. Living in the shadow of Cleveland fed this feeling. Being the country's punchline did not sit well with the ethnic pride of Clevelanders. Ironically, when there was the worst pollution of air and water, there were also the most jobs. Cleveland's Rust Belt economy and mentality held up its people and encouraged their dreams of sending their kids to college. Despite the jokes, Clevelanders had work. Then Japan made a better car and Cleveland suffered and lost.

And the loss surrounding me, and as palpable as sweat in nearly all the stories told by steel pushers and grandparents whose dream for their grandchildren involved little more than "a job with benefits," also fed me as a fledgling writer. Living with pain and loss—by this

I mean, of course, living at all—demands that stories as common as a couple of kids killing a mole be told.

So years later when I read the stories of Raymond Carver and Richard Ford, Bobbie Ann Mason and Jayne Anne Phillips, I recognized the characters in their stories, and I'd already heard stories just as full of meaning.

In my freshman year of college and not long before my mother died of cancer, I walked onto our front porch having just finished reading "The Great Gatsby," written by, perhaps, the most un-working-class American writer alive or dead, with the possible exception of Henry James. But Fitzgerald knew this about working-class Americans: He knew we were capable of dreaming the stories of our lives.

And when I walked onto the porch that night years ago, I dreamed of seeing not Gatsby's but my own green light, the green light that shone for a twelve-year-old boy immigrating to America, the light a friend and I saw emanating from the Chevy plant after a small kill, the light I saw in the eyes of the blue-collar storytellers of my youth. The green light that told the blue-collar story: Go.

Easter's Miracles of Chance

I find it impossible to think of Easter without being reminded of Madalyn Murray O'Hair, the goddess of atheists—a woman my grandparents, aunts and uncles despised for taking God out of the public schools. Playing the role of a destitute American writer, I worked at a series of degrading jobs, that is jobs other than writing, and one of them led me to Ms. O'Hair.

I managed a restaurant in Lexington, Kentucky, where I had the dubious honor of cooking Easter dinner for her and twelve of her disciples at their annual Easter "celebration." While O'Hair celebrated atheism, her son struggled on the street outside, carrying a large wooden cross on his shoulders, more, I believed, in protest of his mother's ostentatious unbelief than in the confirmation of his convictions.

They ate chicken Florentine, drank wine and blasphemed until long after the restaurant had officially closed. Because it was Easter,

I had let all other employees go home early, which left me alone with the pagan thirteen.

About the time she and the twelve had been eating and drinking for an hour after closing, four young women, looking as though they had just returned from spring break in Florida, knocked on the locked door, asking to be let in for dinner. Obeying house rules, I turned them away.

As Mr. O'Hair bellowed for more wine, I watched the spring-break women walk away. Although I am a bedeviled believer, at that moment I couldn't help wondering if these atheists weren't on to something.

(About a month after the O'Hair supper, I quit, or rather forced the crappy crepe place to fire me. If I'd quit, I was contractually bound to repay my moving expenses. The day the crepe place fired me, I'd spent hours at Henry Clay's beloved homestead, Ashland, waiting to be fired, alternately reading *American Heritage* magazine articles on Hemingway and Fitzgerald, and Graham Greene's novel *A Burnt Out Case*.)

Three years later, I spent a few Easter-morning moments with Dick Gregory and John Candy in a Los Angeles bar and restroom, respectively. As Holy Saturday night became early Easter Sunday morning, my brother and I took turns dancing with Gregory's female companion and exchanging quips in the restroom with John Candy. What I remember most is praising Gregory for his essay "Shame" and accusing my brother of attempting to deceive me by saving the $200 we'd vowed to spend.

For the final few months I worked in Washington, D.C., I rented a room in suburban Maryland from an elderly woman who had a boyfriend with a past—he had been a member of the Hitler Youth. The three of us shared an Easter brunch. The discussion moved easily from the whippoorwill to music to 19th Century English poetry.

I covertly studied the man's rolling silver hair and the series of sharp angles that constituted his face. I imagined him as one of the over two million children made to sit at Hitler's feet, to help fight his twisted war. When I asked if he would please pass the strawberry preserves, I searched him for telltale signs of inherent evil. Did it still reside in his hands? Would I be able to see it in his eyes? He offered a small smile as he lifted the sticky jar. I saw nothing save a crumb of bread dangling on the rim of his lower lip. When he and I completed the preserves-passing, all three of us smiled, as if we had just accomplished something significant and lasting. (And maybe we had.) Our toast crunched in a syncopation just short of harmony.

When I look back through the miasma of Easter memories, I locate a young Cleveland boy. He's wearing a new Easter suit and posing, thinking about visiting his grandparents after the ordeal of church, squinting against the sun, standing next to a 1950s-something Plymouth that had somehow earned the childish name the Brown Bunny.

And as I write this, I wonder what miraculous coincidences led this boy to atheists, comedians, and a member of the Hitler Youth, from the Brown Bunny and back, on the temporal stepping-stones of Easter Sundays.

Stop-time #3

Not one of my grandparents, in their late teens and early twenties at the time of the pandemic of 1918, once mentioned the scourge to me or told any stories about those dismal couple of years. They did, however, speak frequently and told endless stories about the two events that did define their lives: The Great Depression and World War II. My paternal grandparents lived in Pennsylvania where sixty thousand people died during the pandemic, which was nearly one tenth of the country's fatalities.

When the Covid-19 pandemic hit us, I at first found solace in the fact that my grandparents did not tell stories of their pandemic. Maybe that meant it wasn't a life-altering concern of theirs. How much did they even know of the pandemic? President Woodrow Wilson deliberately squashed influenza news. He wanted Americans focused on World War I. Plus there were no televisions and no incessant and unending news cycles. I wish now that they had told stories of how they and their loved ones survived the 1918 so-called Spanish Flu. Did they feel the same fears I do? Did they worry about their parents?

Did they dread dying young? I wonder how much the current pandemic will dominate the narrative of my granddaughters' lives.

I have taken solace in the fact that, starting several years before the current pandemic, my two oldest granddaughters, ever prescient, began reading books in the "I Survived" series. They've read 'I Survived the San Francisco Earthquake, 1906" and "I Survived the Sinking of the Titanic, 1912." They've also survived the American Revolution, the eruption of Mount Saint Helens, the destruction of Pompeii, the Great Chicago Fire, the attack of the grizzlies, and the Great Molasses Flood of 1919.

And the books, of course, keep coming.

A Question of Laziness

The dog next door has gone and done it again. All he wanted was to stretch out in the sun on the summer grass and be a damn dog, but the chaos of the invisible electric fence designed to keep him backyard bound interrupted his plans. And worse than that, the current now has him in its electric-shock spell; the dog's howls of pain are second only to the noises emitted from a nearby farm's hog shed in butchering season, noises I believe originate from the ninth circle of hell. If one didn't know about the electric fence, it would appear as if the dog were fighting off the grip of its own madness, an embodiment of spastic, canine chaos. Just when it appears the dog is seconds away from death, his owner runs over and casually kicks him out of the current. I'd like to say here that I empathize with the owner, the hero who saved the life of his dishrag dog too dumb to save himself. I wish I could identify with the wild, free heat of summer or with the raw power and blind force of the electric current. But no. You've probably guessed by now that it is the frightened dog that's still shaking, his hair singed and smoking, with whom I most identify. The creature's turn-down lazy day was thwarted by something he didn't understand and couldn't control, in other words, by real life. That's exactly how I feel more often than I care to admit.

You wouldn't know it to look at me right now, but I'm working on an essay. Sure, it looks like I've got my feet up on my desk, a bowl of pretzels on my lap, a remote in my hand, and an electrified dog on my mind, but I'm working on my essay. That's the beauty of writing an essay on the art and craft of laziness. You're working even when you're not. I'm actually considering writing a twenty-volume cultural history of laziness, which could very well take me the rest of my life, while actually demanding very little of me.

Besides winning the love of a wonderful woman—which I've accomplished—my only other primeval and until now unspoken goal in life has been to achieve a perfect state of laziness. I must say that I don't believe most people who know me consider me lazy, but that's just because either they're not really paying attention or because I'm still trying to accomplish enough in my life so that I may be justifiably lazy, total inertia minus the guilt. Before I can even claim to be nearing the idyllic state of indolence I crave, at minimum I would first need to learn a musical instrument and master a second language. But not every laziness-loving person has these restrictions on his or her condition.

A good friend of mine came home from teaching his writing class one day to find his new son-in-law knocking back a Budweiser and watching TV in the middle of the day with his feet up on the ottoman and his entire right arm immersed in a bag of Ranch Doritos. The man is unemployed and the male member of a shotgun wedding. He's living with my friend—his father-in-law—until he finds a job and gets his feet on the ground, and all the other clichés the world gives lazy people in which to sheath their sloth. This, clearly, is what I deem unearned laziness. If you drop out of high school—or, increasingly, college—don't have a job and are living off your parents, or worse, your in-laws, in my world you're not allowed to be lazy. In fact, I forbid it. Hell, America forbids it. It's lazy people like this who give lazy people like me a bad name. If I found myself in this situation, I would get a job, work hard until I could secure an apartment, save a little money, make sure my spouse was happy, and then look for myriad opportunities for profound laziness.

Lately I've been accruing a list of people who should never be lazy. The list includes illegal immigrants; newly divorced men or women; cancer researchers; strippers; airline pilots; tattooed teenagers, and fat, bald, white guys. Oops. Actually, besides better health, the main reason I want to lose forty pounds is because fat guys can never be lazy. It's against the rules of God and man. It's against my own rules. The combination of fat and lazy just feeds ugly stereotypes, and I refuse to indulge stereotypes about fat, bald guys.

I can't be as lazy as I'd like to be, which is why I get away with the amount of laziness I get away with. How can I really be lazy, right? I worked in construction for years with my father, the living, breathing embodiment of anti-laziness. The man never sits still. Just because the sun happened to rise the other day, my seventy-seven-year-old father decided to spend long hours chopping wood. His never-lazy wife, whom he affectionately calls his sherpa, hauled the wood he chopped. Even my father believes I'm a great worker. He remembers the way I worked while in college, skinny and with long hair, carrying brick and mixing mud, jumping off scaffolding and plunging into piles of sand just for fun. I'd race other laborers to see who could carry stacks of shingles up a ladder and to the peaks of roofs quicker. Even now, when I'm decidedly not college-age or skinny or hirsute, I can still claim having earned three graduate degrees, writing two books, editing a journal and gaining the rank of full professor. Could a lazy person do all that? The answer, of course, is…*I guess so*….Deep down I know how lazy I am, but because I need to achieve a state of earned, guilt-free laziness, I must accomplish more and more. My wife has written 400 books, so I must be exceedingly lazy to have only published two, right? Whenever Dandi and I are sitting at a table with our friends Dan and Barbara, I get this image in my head of a report card containing three As and a B-, and I'm the B-. Type As are never lazy, and I'm nowhere near a type A. If I were ever to win the Pulitzer Prize or the National Book Award for nonfiction, I would never work again. I would leave the house only for the beach. My indolence would be infinite. Dead blowfish washed ashore would accomplish more in an afternoon than I would in a fortnight. And I would use the word fortnight whenever I wanted to, because time would no longer matter to me. Every day would be a fortnight. I wouldn't shave or shower more than a day or two a week, and then only for the sake of health and hygiene. I'm much too lazy to spend my days fighting off contagions. In my worldview, a lazy person must always care for his or her family, of course. How can one enjoy the fruits of true laziness if one's children or grandchildren do not have enough food to eat? You must make sure all your obligations have been met, and then the world of laziness is open to you.

Other people who should never be lazy: A working-class guy who marries a rich woman; the brother-in-law who works for the family business; a trophy wife; my son-in-law; writers I love to read; utility infielders; and the kid who knocked up Sarah Palin's daughter.

According to the Oxford English Dictionary, a lazy person is one "disinclined to work, not disposed to action or effort; idle, inactive, slothful." The second definition is of "a literary style that is languid, having little energy, or later of a river, sluggish, slow-moving." And the third definition is simply, "bad, worthless." Did you know that a lazy-arm "is a type of boom from which a microphone may be hung, or that a lazy dog is a military term for a "fragmentation bomb designed to explode in mid-air and scatter steel pellets at high speed over the target area"? In case we needed it, this is more evidence of the military's deadly disrespect for language. The lazy dog I discussed earlier was closer to a sentence fragment than a bomb fragmenting. Sometimes a slang definition gets it right though. Take the lazy-board, for instance, which is a "short board on the left side of a wagon, used by teamsters to ride on." I like the sound of that.

The word lazy derives from Low Dutch and is synonymous with the much uglier word, sloth. Sloth, of course, is one of the seven deadly sins. Its six siblings are lust, gluttony, greed, wrath, envy and pride. I must admit that I've always had a problem with the seven deadly sins. In many ways they always seemed to me to be relatively lightweight sins, sins bordering on the benign. Why isn't murder one of the seven deadly sins, for instance? Why not rape? Why not invading a country and killing its sovereign leader? Why not war in general? Why not collateral damage? Why not incest? Why not scorning the poor? When I lived in Washington, D.C. in my twenties, a crack-addicted local woman disemboweled her two-year-old son. Why isn't that one of the dreaded seven? I'll take pride over that any day. Now, I understand these sins were cautions to monks, cautions against putting distance between themselves and God. And I can understand this. A monk who's overcome with lust because of a late-afternoon leg shot from a pretty

peasant girl hauling water through the village might have a hard time staying focused on God.

We have the 4th Century monk Evagrius to thank for the seven deadly sins. If he'd had his way, however, there would be eight. His list consisted of gluttony, lust, avarice, sadness, anger, acedia, vainglory and pride. Evagrius did not rank the sins; he believed all sins were committed equal. Two centuries later Pope Gregory knocked out vainglory—which is something I'll despise him for until my dying day—and ruled acedia and sadness redundant. I would love just once in my life to sincerely accuse somebody of vainglory. Unlike Evagrius, Pope Gregory did not believe all sins were equal, so he ranked them from most serious to the least. For Gregory the sin of pride was the worst, lust the least, something for which I'm sure the leg-shot drunk, peasant girl-lusting monk was eternally grateful. Centuries later St. Thomas Aquinas eliminated the idea of ranking sins and restored equality to sinning. Finally, in the 17th Century, sloth replaced sadness and found its rightful place among the seven deadly sins.

Certain people hate being lazy and hate lazy people. My deceased mother was one of these. If she was working in the house, everybody was working. I remember playing baseball in our makeshift ball diamond and seeing her drive by on her way home from the grocery store with bags to unload. She'd lay on her horn as if she were trying to warn my brother and me of an onrushing nuclear winter, all the while pointing toward home. We knew what this meant, of course. "Get home and help me unload these groceries you lazy, baseball-playing losers to whom I had the great misfortune of giving birth." Even though I hated doing it, I loved her, so I'd have to quit the game and head home. I count myself lucky that I married a woman much more like my father than my mother. Dandi could be carrying bulging boxes of books and she'd apologize for blocking my view of the television for two seconds. If she's vacuuming and I'm lying on the floor, she'd be more inclined to outline my body in duct tape as if I were a murder victim than she would ask me to move. With the crime-scene shape of my body outlined on the floor, she could just vacuum that area later on, when I'm, say, stretched out on the couch, watching reruns of the *Rifleman*.

And then there are the people we all wish had been lazy. It's too bad Osama Bin Laden didn't spend his days making his minions perform shadow puppet soap operas on the walls of a cave. Too bad Cossacks didn't kick back more often. What about Nazi concentration camp guards? Colombian death squads? How history would have loved Abraham Lincoln choosing to stay home on that Ford's Theatre night. If I were God, I would have filled the Hutus and Tutsis with every ounce of sloth available to mankind. I'll bet George Armstrong Custer wishes he were just a tad bit lazy. I can imagine a listless, languid Custer staying home to paint Libby's toenails on June 25, 1876. "I really don't feel like doing the whole Battle of the Little Bighorn thing, honey." I'll bet Custer's two brothers, Tom and Boston, their eighteen-year-old nephew, Henry Armstrong Reed, and their brother-in-law, James Calhoun, all four of whom also perished at the Little Bighorn, wish Custer had been as smitten with sloth as he was with ambition. How I wish every guilty person on death row had simply fallen under the spell of old *Tiger Beat* magazines rather than eliminating innocent human beings from the planet. As the late Wendy Wasserstein writes, "…no one was ever murdered or killed in the name of sloth. Furthermore, sloths don't go on religious crusades. Terrorism requires initiative and cunning. If sloths are fundamentalists, their fundamentalist belief is to rest. Hate takes energy. Destroying the ozone layer requires industry. Therefore, slothdom can save humanity."

On a more personal note, I wish my paternal grandfather had been a lazy man. Maybe then he would have decided not to take a walk on that cold November evening, just after dinner and the news. If he'd just been a bit lazy, he might not have collapsed to the ground at his wife's feet, disappearing into the snowy certainty of his fifth and fatal heart attack at the age of sixty-seven. If I could turn back time, I'd want Dandi's cousin Jack to stay back with his men, maybe drink or play cards, maybe catch some shuteye, instead of being brave and ambitious while scouting the ground and losing his life in Vietnam when he was barely eighteen years old. I wish time itself embraced sloth, that it was too lazy to let a perfect-picnic day pass too quickly, or the final moments of a family reunion, or a wedding night, or a childhood summer, or a happy marriage, or a first kiss, or a late-night laugh among friends. How I would love to pray all day, every day, that death, the ever hyperactive, reaper of every grim and lovely thing, would become the king of sloth, the god of inactivity, slumbering through its duties, sleeping every one of its endless years away.

I always need to be careful not to enter the cave of melancholia. I reject the definitions of melancholy that too easily marry it to depression. In my experience melancholy can be…well, I'll just say it: Melancholy can be sorrowfully joyful. Because several dictionaries define it as a pensive or meditative sadness, it is easily differentiated from depression; one is not pensive or meditative when clinically depressed. My favorite definition of melancholy surfaces as the first one in the Shorter Oxford English dictionary: If one is under the spell of melancholia, "[one is] inclined to be sadly thoughtful." And when one is "sadly thoughtful" there is no better place to be than closed off and cozy in a room of one's own, with leather furniture, books and music everywhere, a drum set, more books everywhere, and a stack of DVDs for the moments that dwell just beyond "sadly thoughtful" and promise a soul-feeding story.

I guess I'm not convinced that somebody can be lazy while actively seeking something, even if that something is an escape from the world. Surely entering art in some way, reading a book or listening to music or studying paintings or watching films—in essence seeking the beauty and truth of it all—is in no way lazy. When I have my work done for the day or have at least done all the work that could not be put off until tomorrow or the next day, I hurry to my study, close the blinds, shut off the lights, forage for the perfect film or documentary and move from sadly thoughtful to wistful longing to soul-feeding daydreaming, and then back again, through and around, depending on the scene or story. When I'm in these moods, I can watch only those movies that promise a time or a people long gone. A story with a long-ago ending. Perhaps it's a documentary on the pre-Colombian Indians or the American Civil War. If it's a film, I want it to be historic in nature. Not only does watching the movie *Gettysburg* make me feel less lazy because I can claim to be learning—hell maybe even studying—American history, but certain moments in the film feed me like very few other things do. Grading five more papers will not feed my soul. Nor will paying bills or exercising or cutting my lawn. But what will is one moment of Joshua Lawrence Chamberlain, colonel of the 20th Maine, talking to his men the day before the battle of Gettysburg begins. I almost have to brace myself for the moment so as not to cry, which is why I always watch movies like this with a blanket nearby and a pillow under my head. Each time I brace myself and each time, without fail, Chamberlain says, "we are an army out to set other men free," and each time I tear up because I have just heard something good and true and beautiful. This moment helps me remain separate from some other contemporary lies about armies and their motives. When Chamberlain speaks, I feel connected to life as it should be, to time long gone and to people who suffered and loved and dreamed and prayed and buried and remembered, and lived on, just as we do.

So am I really lazy for watching *Gettysburg* for the thirtieth time, or am I just a beast on a leather couch, dabbing his tears with a blanket, being nurtured and nourished by narrative, being sustained like only story can sustain us? Because that's what I'm in search of finally; I'm seeking a different story than the one I'm living that day, a new narrative. A counter-narrative to the one being told by an administration, or a dictator, or a terrorist. And while there's no doubt there's an escapist element to my leather-couch laziness, I escape the world only to reenter it better than I was before, believing that despite all the evidence to the contrary, for instance, once in a great while, or once upon a time, armies fought "to set other men free."

My retreat is akin to asking the universe to tell me a story. The essayist Scott Russell Sanders understands the universal stories I'm talking about when he writes, "Stories...help us to see through the eyes of other people; show us the consequences of our actions; educate our desires; help us dwell in place [and time]; help us deal with suffering, loss and death; teach us how to be human; and acknowledge the wonder and mystery of creation." Too often I need to be reminded of these things. I'm ashamed to admit that there are times when the mild stress of a difficult morning corrodes my capacity for empathy, when I forget what it means to be human, what it really means, not what Wall Street or Madison Avenue or St. Peter's Square or Main Street tells me it means. And worst of all, too often I fail to be awed by the "wonder and mystery of creation." I worry about that one most of all, so I'm always on guard, especially in early fall, when caterpillars migrate across country roads at speeds too slow to calculate. Why not just stay where you were? I want to ask them. If I see their migration as foolish and futile rather than wondrous and grand, I rush up to my office, close the blinds, grab my blanket and watch as a story unfolds, where, for instance, a young, 19th Century Pennsylvania couple packs up all their belongings into a Conestoga wagon and heads west, reminded not only of the wonder of migrations great and small, but of what it is to dream. Or perhaps on a rainy Wednesday afternoon I need a story about a late-18th Century French trapper on the Great Plains or in the shadow of the Colorado Rockies who saves the life of an aging Arapahoe man and makes a friend for life. Or perhaps it's a movie set in the Victorian age when people talked of God and belief unapologetically and unabashedly, without these beliefs being used to justify heaping horror on all who believe differently.

And if I'm lucky and if I've been paying attention and if the story was a good one, I'll be kicked out of the electrical current of my own mini-madness, the madness that tells me my story's all about 401(k)s and water cooler talk, or that it's all about building more bombs, or the right kind of tennis shoes, or about spending freezes across the board, or about having the post-fifty sports car, or the pre-thirty woman, or the giant lie that all I have is not enough. Stories, the ones that feed me when I'm lazy, are always and ultimately about the power of love and peace and family and friends and hope and dreams and suffering and loss and yes, even death, which won't embrace sloth soon enough for any of us.

Stop-time #4

Not long after Cosimo landed in New York City, a twelve-year-old boy in South Fork, Pennsylvania was pulled out of school by his father and forced to join him in the rough area's coal mines. His father had pulled him out of school when he turned nine. Whenever I heard my father tell of his father becoming a coal miner in the ninth grade, I've imagined my great-grandfather, known as Pap, walking down the hallway of an elementary school in South Fork, his hands caked in coal dust, his eyes in a squint, having trouble adjusting to the school's artificial light. He spends a minute or two with the principal. It doesn't take long. The principal's seen this drama before, knows it's a mineral-hard reality of life in South Fork, where streets are so steep it's an arduous trek reaching one's home. A family needs the money more than the boy needs the education. I see my grandfather, Russell, looking up from his books and seeing his father standing just outside the door. The principal apologizes for interrupting the class. Russell's teacher turns to the boy. The boy notices his father. He can almost see the dirt on his fingers, even smell the stench of the mines. At first his father's presence seems oddly out of context. But then he knows; his time has come. He pushes himself out of his desk, pockets a pencil, and moves toward the front of the classroom, where his teacher, his principal, his father, and his future wait.

Of course, chances are it didn't happen this way. I no longer have any way of really knowing. My version owes more to the literal mindedness of youth than to the verifiable facts of history. I'm sure that one night after supper, after rolling and smoking a cigarette, exterminating the butt in the saucy remains of his supper plate, Pap broke the news to his son. The next day my grandfather entered the mine. His job was to guide the mule in and out, down and then out, deeper into the earth and then out again. I imagine Russell studying the coal-encrusted hair of the beast, searching its eyes for signs of life, a dream life perhaps, about hooves in fertile fields and head bent to soft grass.

There were weeks when miners saw the sun only on the Sabbath.

On a website dedicated to Pennsylvania miners, bagpipes pump out "Amazing Grace" as a visitor learns that since 1870, thirty years before Russell's birth, over fifty thousand miners died from mining accidents, over thirty thousand in anthracite mines, twenty thousand in bituminous. Clicking away from the site strikes me cold: grace one second, none the next.

Russell's time in the coal mines carved out a groove in my father's vision for his oldest son's future. My father allowed no discussion of his children not attending college, knowing an education was the way up and out of work with a bent back.

I've also heard stories of Russell walking home from fourteen hours in the mine and of a headstrong little girl, his age, who'd asked him how much he'd made that day. I believe he saw the girl's question more impertinent than flirtatious. I'm sure it must have contained some of both. This young girl, Marie Casey, was nothing if not headstrong and pragmatic. At my younger brother's high school graduation party, twelve years after her husband's death and ten months before her own, she looked on in disgust when she saw alcohol being served. She despised alcohol—never imbibed in her life—and never trusted the way it warped people. People like her paternal grandfather who, walking home from a hillside bar in the early morning of a coal-black night, took a short cut across railroad tracks and was killed by a train, leaving his distraught wife and oldest son to raise eight children. I'm sure if she would have seen Russell sipping one drink, she would have ignored him on his walks away from the coal mines and my father would not have been born and the rest of this, the all of it—the stuff and story at the hands of fate or God or accident or chaos depending on one's beliefs—would never have happened. But it all, somehow, miraculously did.

The Teacher

I often wonder what kind of man I'd be if I'd been home to answer the phone that day. I imagine my ex-wife's frustration and mounting anxiety with each unanswered ring. She must have found a quick and quiet place to make the call. She probably heard him rampaging around the front room or kitchen, his lungs filled with dope, veins rigid with rage. What was Carol thinking as her new husband threatened to beat her and kill me?

Carol had married J.D. a month before the missed phone call and all that was soon to follow. Before the wedding day, he'd attempted to force the ringed symbol of their union down her narrow throat; her veins pushed against her skin like strained roots. Despite everyone's pleas for her to leave, Carol stayed, as many battered women do, beaten beyond courage, frightened to the point where instincts turn inward in a kind of masochistic survival.

She and my son spent the next five months living with a man they soon hated, a man who beat my ex-wife, frightened my son, and killed the man I thought I was.

Carol and I had been divorced for several years. Through a comfortable rhythm of visitation and child support, rights acknowledged, and responsibilities accepted, daily phone calls and every other Christmas, we'd become friends. A friendship her violent husband could not understand.

I missed her phone call that day. The call intended to warn me to stay away from her house because her husband had threatened my life and intended to complete his promise when I dropped off my son on that simple, sunny, Sunday afternoon.

Because I was to spend the next four months in Oklahoma before returning to Ohio, my son and I spent that whole day playing two-man baseball, football, basketball, trying to fit the sports of distant seasons into the hours of an afternoon.

An hour before we were to meet Carol at her house, my son Danny asked if we could open my briefcase, the briefcase never used for business but whose sole purpose was to hold and preserve the hundreds of pictures he'd drawn for me since he was old enough to cradle a crayon between thumb and index finger. He began counting all the artwork he'd created for me in our six years together. I'd kept everything, hundreds of them, one or two at a time. The collection began with nothing more than a blank page with a single line drawn down the center, created by my son when all he could do to claim a piece of the world was to run a black crayon down a white page. As he aged, his work progressed. Animals and football players soon followed, as did our longtime favorites, the deep-sea divers, their wire-mesh masks obscuring their faces, their leather skins protecting them from the dangers of the depths they descended.

As I sat next to my son on the couch, looking at a fraction of all he had given me, guilt suddenly and quietly descended, its weight accumulating one feather at a time until a bird of iron sat hunched on my shoulders, pecking at the entrails of an idealized fatherhood. I'd be gone for the next four months, I told him, then home for Christmas, gone again, and then home for good.

I didn't say goodbye to him at that moment. I'll do it as late as possible, I told myself; that way the memory will last longer, long into the time we'll be apart, the time he'll be living with his mother and with the man with initials for a name who would soon change all our lives.

What we talked about on the drive to Carol's house I do not remember. I'm sure I tried to put a positive spin on my departure and his mother's doomed marriage. The goodbye I'd held all day, I'm holding still.

When we reached my ex-wife's house, I pulled to the curb, love-brushed my son's hair with my hand, told him I loved him; his tiny echo followed. Before I reached Danny's side of the car, I heard the screen door slam behind me. When I looked over my shoulder, the stranger who lived with my son stood no more than fifteen feet away from me. Rage pinned his skin to the bones and muscles of his face. "Go in the house, pal. I'll see you in a minute," I said to my son in a voice I tried to modulate just right in order to keep the panic to myself. Whether sensing something in my voice or simply wanting to obey the final order I'd give him for a few months, Danny hurried into the house, his suitcase banging against his leg, the left side of the body leaning, trying to balance the weight of his baggage.

"I'm going to kick your ass right here," the initial-man said, taking two huge steps in my direction.

I didn't move. I couldn't.

As if my peripheral vision sensed something it wanted me to see, I glanced at the picture window and saw the worried faces of my ex-wife and our son; his face seemed to glow as if a halo had risen behind him. That light, I deduced later, was nothing more than the unlikely product of sunlight and tears. The glistening sheen of sadness.

The man I knew only by his initials stood well over six feet tall. His body nothing more than a sculpture of muscle. A too handsome face. An unidentifiable tattoo writhed on his right bicep as he pointed his finger in my face. He delivered invectives speckled with obscenities, accusing me of sleeping with my ex.

I vowed that if he touched me, I wouldn't stop fighting until one of us could fight no more. But the second I made this vow to the animal side of my self, I knew I couldn't let it happen. I wouldn't let my son watch his father fight. I refused to teach him the lesson that men settled problems with blood and fists. Even though they did exactly that. Even though it is the way of men and nations, always has been, always would be, despite what happened on this small square of lawn. If the man hits me, I decided, I'll let him. I'll crawl to the police station and press charges before I let myself become the kind of man I am not.

"So why do you keep calling her? What is it with you two?" he asked, still pointing a finger out of an otherwise clenched fist. I focused on his finger. The more I looked at it, the more grotesquely mutant it became, changing color, shape, size, finally resembling something like the leg of a fetus protruding from a rock.

"You're divorced ain't you? I don't even talk to my ex-wives."

Ex-wives. Plural.

It was then I sensed an opening.

"It must be hard having your kids in another state," I said. The rock and fetus disappeared.

What else I said to calm this lunatic down I do not remember. I must have stayed away from the war words I was thinking. While I uttered one banal and embarrassing complacency after another, my mouth must have resembled a cavern whose walls were covered with covert obscenities. After a few more threats, the stranger with initials for a name returned to his house, his wife. My son.

Although I've re-imagined this confrontation many times, I cannot recall more of its details. Other dialogue and description have become spots on a window, spots I've been trying to rub away by somehow wiping the wrong side of the glass. The details reside where the truth is, the truth I've been avoiding, the truth I've stuck on the other side of the event.

The truth is this: I was scared. Scared into the clichés of a group of twelve-year-old boys. Whenever I've told the story of that Sunday afternoon, even if performing the twin roles of speaker and participant, I've told only one side of the truth. That day, I vowed what I had always vowed whenever facing a battle of fists and flesh: I will talk my way out of it. That I would say anything, do anything, promise anything, disavow anything. Wait for the cock to crow for the third time. I remember standing in my street as a thirteen-year-old. For whatever reason a fight had been arranged. I was there; he was there. Out of the corner of my eye I saw my dad take a seat on our front porch, there to intervene only if severe injury seemed imminent. Perhaps he sat there as a way of encouraging me, or perhaps he watched for the same reasons my wife and son watched twenty years later. Curiosity? Or hope? To see his son, her ex-husband, his father become a man? But what kind of man? What I did that day twenty years ago was whisper to the kid that my dad was watching him. The fight never happened. The kid rode away. I don't remember the lie I told my father.

Now, when I watch my son applauding fights at hockey games, cheering baseball brawls, or telling me with pride how he returned a punch in the playground, I understand that a part of him wanted me to pound that sociopath into the ground on that lovely Sunday afternoon. Perhaps my father wanted to see the same thing so long ago.

The next day, as scheduled, I left for Oklahoma. As I drove, I fought the urge to turn around, drive back, plow my car through the picture window, reclaim what was no longer mine, and the person who always would be. Homicidal rage seethed, surfacing from the safe distance of time and separation. While driving through Indiana I bludgeoned this guy to death with a crowbar. In Illinois, driving past acres and miles of tar-black, fecund soil, I cut the brake line of his truck, watched as the truck rounded a dangerous curve, busted through a guardrail, plummeted over a cliff, tumbling, finally exploding in a prime-time TV blaze. I imagined blood-covered baseball bats, hockey sticks, the burnt smell of a warm gun. Happiness is indeed a warm gun, I might have screamed.

And then, midway through Missouri, as I glanced at the flick of a Herford's tail, I sobbed, partly in anger, partly in longing, partly out of sorrow for my son, but mostly, I realize now, I sobbed because I wanted nothing more in life at that moment on a clear and fair Missouri morning than to end the life of another human being. A couple hundred miles west of St. Louis, I understood that I'd crossed the line and become the second of the two types of people in the world: the type capable of murder.

I knew then that I could kill. For thirty years I'd lived with the certain knowledge that even if forced to war, I would not take the life of another human being. I imagined myself lying face down on a battlefield feigning death until all fighting men moved to other battles. Then I would get up. And run.

But I now know differently.

I have since relinquished my status as conscientious objector and have become a spiritual brother of Cain and his countless descendants. A pacifist no longer, I've lived as a could-be killer now for eight years.

Several months after the incident in my son's front yard, the phone rang in my Oklahoma kitchen. My ex-wife had called with the prayed-for information that she'd left the wife beater with initials in place of a name. She cried while telling me that he'd destroyed our son's collection of glass animals. I imagined the shards of a thousand species strewn on a bedroom floor, each somehow defying extinction, each still somehow capable of catching and holding a hint of light.

At times, and in oddly the same way I believe I see my dead mother or an old lover in a crowd, I mistake the face of a stranger for the man with initials for a name. When I do, my first instinct is to flee, leaving him and the memory of his violence a part of the past that creeps into the present only through the miasmas of my son's occasional nightmares and in the awareness of the man I now know myself to be. Or I consider a frontal attack, my non-calloused hands clamped around his neck, my thumbs digging into his Adam's apple until he chokes to death on the bump that distinguishes him as a man.

But at other times, times I'm feeling more reflective, when I'm feeling humble enough to face the truth, when I'm feeling secure and serene enough to believe self-knowledge is indeed a supreme gift, I imagine myself walking up to him, reaching my hand out to his, and then thanking him, my enemy, my teacher, this violent man who taught me the ugly truth about who I am.

Stop-time #5

My paternal grandparents, Marie and Russell, dated and then were engaged for ten years. Ten long years they waited because Marie was Catholic, and Russell was not. Marie's mother vowed not to attend her daughter's wedding if she went ahead with it. Marie and Russell did get married after a decade of courtship and promise. Marie's mother stayed home.

How much do we carry of those who have gone before us?

Words of My Youth

I stand at the edge of my suburban driveway on Fairlawn Drive, sunned and safe. My friend Mick and I play Whiffle ball. Each swing of the bat sends the ball flying into the mystery grip of physics and aerodynamic wonder. The ball appears headed straight up before some hidden hand of wind and speed and serrated plastic jerks it over to the lawn of the widow next door. Mrs. Worth's boxer drools the day away, watching from the backyard in its own state of ignorant awe. We take turns "smacking the shit" out of the plastic ball. I don't notice, not right away, an older kid—a man really—walking down the other side of the street, his eyes straight ahead. Not from around here. As the kid-man gets closer, I focus more intently on the game, as if this focus will protect me from what's about to happen. I chase the ball as if catching it matters more than anything, more than my first kiss or my last day of school. I make careful throws, keeping my eye on the ball, trying to anticipate the direction of its flight and fall. I fear—as I so often fear—that something I have done has found its way back to me. And now I'll pay. Five or six houses away now, the kid-man crosses the street. He's not from around here, but I recognize him from somewhere. There's something in the way the kid-man never looks around, as if his entire world centers on a horizon only he can see. He's smoking. Not a good sign. I pick the ball up off the boxer's drool-wet lawn, wipe the drool on my jeans, and toss it a few feet in the air. When I look up, I see the kid-man—black hair greased and straight, a broken mustache, patches of dirt and beard—punch Mick in the nose. Mick bends over and covers his nose with cupped hands in one motion. Blood oozes through his summer-stained fingers and drips onto the hot cement. Although the kid-man— eighteen, nineteen, probably—has just punched Mick in the face, I'm stunned stupid when the kid-man walks over to me and slams me in the nose. We run to the porch.

"My girlfriend's not a dyke," the kid-man says, as he lights a new cigarette from the old and walks off.

It's true. We have called the man's girlfriend a dyke. Often and repeatedly. But still, standing behind the harsh-sounding, cool-sounding word with blood dripping from my nose, I, who only a minute ago was playing Whiffle ball on a summer afternoon, realize I cannot define, nor do I understand the word we all so love to use.

Again on the Whiffle ball driveway, also summer, also my twelfth year, I call one of my Gentile friends a dumb Jew. Soon all of us revel in the discovery of this new slur. This new way of degrading each other catches on quickly. Not one of the Catholic boys schooled in the Judeo-Christian tradition is sure why calling somebody a dumb Jew is derogatory. But we celebrate this new slur anyway. But wait.

Wasn't Jesus a Jew? Isn't our friend Bill Rosenberg a Jew? We all love Bill. This must be something else. It sounds different. It sounds like it shouldn't be said. So we say it and love saying it, we boys without weapons.

The screen door slams. My mother has caught the sound of the slur. She motions for me to come inside. "Tell your friends to go home," she says.

I do not have to. They're gone. This is 1971, and the suburbs. Somebody's parent is everybody's parent. Parents stick together. They know who the real enemy is.

She grabs my hair and pulls me into the house. Inside my head I'm screaming.

I do not say a word.

"What did you say out there? What were you saying?"

I understand that my mother knows the answer to her questions. I realize I had better not repeat what I said outside, not even in answer to her questions. I know she never wants to hear that again. Not ever. Not from me. Not from anybody.

"Where did you ever hear a thing like that? That kind of talk?" she asks.

An excellent question. I honestly do not know. I have no idea. The slur just seems to have been out there, there and somehow not there, like incense, like the way a Whiffle ball whips and dips, the way adults laugh at things kids don't understand, the way background noise from a baseball game leaks out of transistor radios, the way factory fires flirt with the night sky, the way sonic booms burst the lie of silence.

By Force, Threat, or Deception

On Friday the thirteenth, just twelve days before his forty-second birthday, a birthday he swore he'd never see, Don pulled out of his parking space at a job he hated and turned into eastbound traffic. As he headed down Detroit Avenue to one of his favorite bars, he turned on his headlights to combat the disappearance of daylight, on one of those winter afternoons when darkness comes before supper, when evening subsumes late afternoon, when all that is known of daytime bows to the early night.

As he drove toward the Driftwood Inn through the rain and snow, mixed and falling, perhaps Don thought of ways to spend the paycheck neatly folded in his wallet, or of his dream of becoming a painter; or maybe he conjured up images of his past: of his time as a dance instructor at Arthur Murray's, guiding couples through the steps of the waltz or the gyrations of the jitterbug, or of his time in the service during the Korean War. Or maybe thoughts of his recent past crept into his mind with the stealth and skill of a cancer cell: of his leaving his kind wife and doomed marriage of twelve years, the look on the face of the ten-year-old daughter he loved as he drove away from their home, to his new home five miles away, with his belongings carefully packed in the truck of his Lincoln Continental.

He had popped in the bar merely to have a drink and cash his check. Bars did that then. Maybe some still do. While he was in the bar, Don no doubt talked easily to strangers; he was friendly, well-liked by men and women. Especially women. They could always talk to him. And his dark brown hair, aquiline nose, easy manner and penchant for dressing above his means seemed to draw women to him. On this day maybe he bought a few drinks for friends, feeling that familiar working-class flush of Friday riches: riches tentative, hard won, well-deserved, riches here on Friday afternoon and gone on Monday morning.

When Don walked to his car, having stayed no more than an hour, just long enough to get out of the cold, have a warm drink, enjoy the reflection of himself in a barroom mirror, he made the mistake of letting strangers see his wad of money. As he braced against the light breeze blowing in off Lake Erie, two young men—two Hispanic kids, Spanish or Puerto Rican—surprised him. One pushed a gun in Don's back and forced him into his car.

The men wound up at the northwestern edge of Edgewater Park in Cleveland at a place called Perkins Beach, where the lake became part of the night. Lake Erie's latent waves crashed and fell against the rocky shore of Edgewater Park. The temperature hovered just above freezing. The older kid, who did all the talking, got in the passenger seat; the other kid hopped in the back. The boy in back was only sixteen.

The punk sitting shotgun pointed a .38 in Don's face.

"Hand over the money or I'll kill you," the punk said.

Don lunged for the gun. The kid fired.

For years this was the story the family believed. A convenient story. Ugly, but safe. Horrible, but ordinary. But it wasn't the whole truth.

Somehow I always knew much of what happened to my uncle had become a family fiction. Maybe it was the way the story never changed, as if one detail out of place would cause the entire narrative edifice to come tumbling down, resembling a collapsed cathedral, its glory betrayed by the sudden clutter of its bricks. It could have been the way my father, a former Cleveland homicide detective and my uncle's good friend, mysteriously lost interest in the case. He simply didn't want to know anything he didn't want to know.

I, however, have never been able to let it go. I've encouraged the family to talk about it. Not because I thought it would do any of us any good, but because aspects of my uncle's murder had been mired in mystery for so long that rumors and innuendo had begun to seep into holes of doubt. I needed to know more. For twenty-five years I have remained selfishly, seriously curious. I am now the age my uncle was when he died. I'm probably not even entitled to dig around in the ruins of my uncle's murder. We were not bound by blood but by marriage. He taught me how to play tennis; he talked to me often and always treated me well, assuring me that when it came to women,

I wouldn't have a problem. As an awkward and unhappy teenager, I appreciated the apparent sincerity and wisdom of his words.

I know I loved him, and I'm hoping this love is enough to attempt to tell his story.

You're at Uncle Don's house not long after he and your aunt separated. You watch the maroon Lincoln Continental pull in the driveway. You see him kiss his ten-year-old daughter goodbye. (Was it the last time he ever saw her? She him?) You run through the kitchen and down the steps. When your aunt sees you she asks where you're going. You tell her you want to talk to Uncle Don. "You don't have to," she says, picking up a laundry basket filled with women-only whites. "Okay," you say, hearing something in her words you feel you should obey. You turn your back on the door that leads to him. You never see your uncle again.

The night after the murder, my uncle's smiling face from better times appeared boxed in the corner of the TV screen. The newscaster mispronounced his polysyllabic Polish surname. After a day or two his picture was replaced with an icon meant to represent murder in the abstract: a cartoon-like drawing of a gun superimposed on a chalk sketch of a body strewn on a street, a faceless, nameless body. It could have been anybody. Which it was. Which it wasn't.

In order for members of my family to get at what really happened twenty-five years ago this fall, we'd have to give up at least a modicum of the memory of the man we thought we knew. We'd have to take a fresh look at the man we called husband, brother-in-law, father, friend. The man I called Uncle Don. And, finally, we'd all have to learn a little something about a few strangers—strangers even to my uncle. We'd also have to get to know a guy named Alan G. Barnes.

You have appointed yourself the person who has to get at the truth. After twenty-five years, you still believe the truth is out there. In buried police reports and in the distant memories of aging detectives. In secret, stolen family moments. In the hidden history of people you claim to love. You want to tell your uncle's story. No matter what. Why is it so important that you know what happened? Who are you to believe you have a right to the truth—or even the facts?

On Friday the thirteenth, just twelve days before his forty-second birthday, a day he swore he'd never see, Don—whose father died at forty-one—pulls out from his parking space at Alan Pack and Rubber Co. and away from the steeple-shadow of the Methodist church on the corner, which must have hovered over him on this day the way the Catholic Church had his entire life. As he turns into eastbound traffic and heads down Detroit Ave. to one of his favorite bars, he switches on his headlights and settles into the leather seats of his Lincoln.

As he drives toward the Driftwood Inn through the rain and snow, mixed and falling, perhaps Don calculates the division of his paycheck, wondering how much he'd have left after debts and other bills. Surely enough for the extra gas for the long, out-of-the-way drive to Perkins Beach.

Alan G. Barnes also felt the promise of Perkins, albeit in a more sinister way. Barnes must have been feeling the oncoming weight of his twentieth birthday, which at the time of his becoming a murderer was only three days away. Perhaps he foresaw his dimly lit future, which looked a lot like his present. He was nineteen years old, living in his parents' W. 87 St. Cleve- land home; he had minimal education, no job, and a shared, fledgling criminal enterprise with a sixteen-year-old who would soon become his accomplice in a kidnapping and murder.

But Barnes had stumbled onto something interesting and potentially profitable back in August of 1974 when he'd assaulted his first victim; and it was then he must have begun noticing the population frequenting Perkins Beach. It was the same population that frequented other Cleveland hot spots like West 25th, West 32nd (where the gay bath houses sat), West 45th, West 65th. Barnes viewed the gays who congregated at these spots as easy marks. A lot of them were married. Even if they weren't married, they didn't want to report to the police that they had been cruising when robbed. A lot of people could not care less what befell homosexuals. They probably asked for it anyway. They were the perfect marks.

Some members of the Cleveland and Lakewood police departments even had a name for Barnes and those with a similar modus operandi: "tulip vultures." Barnes quickly became a tulip vulture extraordinaire. Although Barnes lived in Cleveland, the then sixty-four-year-old city of Lakewood began only thirty blocks from his house, and even in the early 1970s, the city was known as the "flower patch." Just five miles west of Cleveland's downtown sat what was once a forest along Lake Erie, now a city fertile with homosexuals, mostly male. And near the border of Lakewood and Cleveland sat Perkins Beach, which already had a reputation as a lovers' lane, a place where gays could hook up, hang out and avoid being hassled by the police.

The border separating the two cities was symbolic as well as geographical, serving as a dividing line between decent living and decadence, moving up or going down. The Cleveland police were too busy with homicides (over three hundred a year at the time) and other big-city crime; and neighboring Lakewood police had an arrangement with the city's large homosexual population, which in 1974 was just over twenty thousand "card-carrying homosexuals" in a city of around seventy thousand. The arrangement, simply stated, was: "We won't bother you guys, but don't lie to us. If you're cruising and get beat up, just say that. Don't make up a big story that's impossible for us to believe."

Perhaps because they were left alone by the police and didn't want to jeopardize that relationship, or their marriages, or their reputations, more than ninety percent of gay victims of crime never filed reports.

With all this in his favor, Barnes figured he was onto something good. He assumed that at five feet ten inches tall and a hundred and seventy pounds, young and lithe, with brown hair and hazel eyes, the correct moves and the right clothes, he just might be able to make this work.

It's bad enough you have to pry into your uncle's life, but you soon learn that to discover what happened to him, you'll have to investigate a string of robberies committed by the murderer just prior to the murder. And in the robbery reports are the names of other victims. Were they all lured by the unspoken promises of Perkins Beach? Suddenly you're reading the names of others, names, attached to men, men attached to lives and families. In at least one case you'll know more than his wife and family ever knew about a particular autumn day. You wonder if you know more than your aunt does. You worry about the talk you'll soon have to have with her.

Michael McEntee was ten years out of college. He had a wife and two young children, a good job in Cleveland, and an urge he couldn't control. At least he couldn't control the urge on November 1, 1974.

McEntee left downtown Cleveland at 1 p.m. and headed west. He later told the police he wanted to grab lunch at the Blue Fox, a restaurant that for a generation had served fine dinners and businessmen lunches on the boundary of Cleveland and Lakewood. But he needed some cash first, so he pulled up in the auto teller line at Cleveland Trust for some lunch money.

Enjoying a free hour, McEntee cranked up the car radio as he waited in line. He wasn't in line very long when a guy without a weapon jerked open the driver's door and pushed McEntee hard on the left shoulder, so he'd move to the passenger seat. The perp got behind the wheel.

"Give me your wallet," he said.

The perp took McEntee's wallet. Disappointed by the few dollars he stole, the guy eventually forced McEntee to write several checks.

Detective Michael Flynn of the Lakewood Police Department couldn't understand why a guy looking to rob somebody would choose a car sitting in an auto teller line, where the car could easily be trapped.

"I remember talking to this guy [McEntee]," Flynn said twenty-five years later as he looked over the police report, running his fingers through his thinning gray hair. "I knew I was being hosed. I knew he had cruised somewhere. He had to have been at Perkins."

Flynn remembers McEntee making a composite of the suspect. He remembers him mentioning several times that he was married.

Detective Flynn, whose still handsome, angular face and mustache conjure images of former TV cops, knew it was time to ask the question he'd been holding back.

"Why did you pull off at Perkins Beach?"

McEntee wouldn't answer.

"Are you a homosexual?" Flynn asked, his experience telling him that crime at Perkins Beach always involved homosexuals.

"I'm a heterosexual," McEntee said. "I told you. I'm married."

At this time Flynn brought up the possibility of McEntee taking a polygraph test.

Flynn waited.

"One time. In college. A group of us from Ohio State went out and had a homosexual commit fellatio on us," McEntee said.

Flynn waited. He wanted to leave McEntee a respectable out.

"I'd like to change one thing in my story, and then I'll take a polygraph."

McEntee informed Flynn that the crime did initiate at Perkins Beach, not in an auto teller line.

McEntee left downtown Cleveland at 1 p.m. and headed west. He wanted to grab lunch at the Blue Fox. Instead of going to lunch, however, McEntee decided to waste a little time at Perkins Beach, maybe catch a little shut eye before heading back to work. He drove his gray 1971 Camaro up the long road leading past Edgewater Park and into the more secluded Perkins Beach area.

He draped his suit jacket over the back of the passenger seat, undid his top shirt button, loosened his tie, leaned his back against the driver's door and stretched his legs across the Camaro's console. Finally, he dozed off.

Suddenly McEntee jerked awake. Some guy ripped open the driver's door and grabbed McEntee's arm with one hand and his tie with the other.

"Move over," the guy demanded.

McEntee scrambled to the passenger seat.

Barnes, clean-shaven and neatly dressed in brown from his zipper-down shirt to suede zippered boots, hurried behind the wheel and threw McEntee's suit jacket into his lap.

"Give me your wallet," Barnes said.

McEntee removed his wallet from his jacket and handed his money, eleven dollars, to Barnes. Barnes took the wallet, checked it out and handed it back.

"You got a checkbook, right?" Barnes asked. "Then write a check for fifty dollars. Where's the closest auto teller?"

McEntee told Barnes where he could cash the check.

With McEntee still in the passenger seat, Barnes left Perkins Beach and drove east along the Cleveland Shoreway. Frustrated by construction, Barnes turned and took an alternate route, pounding the Camaro over a dirt road filled with holes. As he drove, Barnes flipped through McEntee's checkbook.

"Is the balance in here right?" Barnes asked.

"No."

"Write another check for fifty dollars."

"Why?"

"Because of that," Barnes said as he pointed to another branch of Cleveland Trust bank.

McEntee wrote another check for fifty dollars.

"When can I get out of the car?" McEntee asked.

"In a couple of minutes. Write another one for two hundred dollars," Barnes said as the Camaro idled in the Cleveland Trust auto teller line. Barnes took both checks and edged up in line.

"It's dumb to have two checks because they'll only cash one of them," McEntee told Barnes, either because he was trying to win him over or because he was frightened of what might happen if the bank refused to cash the checks.

Barnes agreed, ripping the smaller check into tiny pieces and tossing the scraps in the car's ashtray.

Losing patience, Barnes suddenly began pounding on the horn and rocking the car back and forth as he tried to get out of line. When he managed to escape the line, Barnes darted to the front and parked right by the lobby.

When Barnes informed McEntee that they were going inside the bank to cash the check, McEntee figured this would be the best time to get away. He too got out of the car and walked in front of Barnes into the bank. "Look at the crowd," McEntee said when he opened the bank door.

"Get in the car," Barnes shouted. "Get back in the car or else!"

McEntee opened the car door as if to get in, but then he slammed the door and ran into the bank.

Barnes started the car and drove away, the dual white walls on the Camaro's front tires blurring in the afternoon. The police later found the car in the parking lot of a Cleveland bar.

"The only reason this guy filed a report is because the check was out there, and he knew he'd have to tell his wife something," Flynn said. "He had to come up with an explanation. If it was money only, we'd have never heard from him."

You recall your recent conversation with McEntee's wife. "My husband died four years ago," she said. "Cancer. He was only fifty-one. I don't think I want to talk about this over the phone. For all I know you could be the guy who did it. Anyway, I don't think I can tell you anything about your uncle's murder," she tells you. "All I know is that my husband was in line at an auto teller and the guy jumped in his car."

You thank her and tell her you will not call again.

Over the next six weeks, Barnes picked up his pace. Shortly after the McEntee kidnapping and the bungled check-cashing scheme, Barnes kidnapped Thomas Walker on November 12 under similar circumstances. He abducted Michael J. Palmison on December 4 and Alan W. Rounds on December 11. All of these men were picked up in or around Perkins Beach. All of them had been taken "by force, threat or deception."

Don pushes the accelerator down as he picks up his speed, driving faster now, hard. As he drives toward Perkins, he passes apartment buildings built in English Tudor style, and cruises beneath the shade of the maples and oaks lining Clifton Blvd., which once was home to Cleveland's wealthy families of industry.

Although Don at times may have lived as if he were from a wealthy family, he was not. With only a high school education, he had worked as an elevator repairman, a street sweeper, a shipping clerk. For a time he even trafficked in cigarettes. Don would drive his Lincoln down to North Carolina where he'd pull up in front of a barn at 3 a.m. The barn door opened, and he drove in. Immediately the door shut behind him and lights went on. Without much being said, three or four guys would load the Lincoln with one thousand cartons of cigarettes, ensuring that not a single carton showed above window level. Don would pay the sellers one dollar a carton in North Carolina, drive back to Ohio and sell them for two dollars a carton when cartons regularly sold for four dollars. The only tax that went unpaid was the

Ohio tax, so it looked to be a good gig. Unfortunately, Don never had money in his hands for long. Instead of turning around with the one thousand dollars profit and going back for another cache, Don blew the money and had to borrow cash from friends and family in order to make another run, which was why the paycheck stub found in his wallet on the day of his death was for two hundred and eighty-two dollars for two weeks of work.

Don doesn't stay long at the Driftwood Inn, just long enough to get out of the cold, feel the wet heat of Cutty Sark, enjoy his reflection in a barroom mirror, and cash his check.

No minorities—no Spanish or Puerto Ricans—spotted a wad of money. Barnes waits miles away, eating chicken and holding a gun.

You once watched Uncle Don wash his wife's hair, carefully brushing it out, blowing it dry, gently foraging through it with his fingers as if searching for the secret of the static electricity he created. Her hair billowed. He was electric; he had the touch. As he brushed his wife's hair, he had everything in its place: brush here; gel there, comb here. Twice you playfully rearranged his tools. The second time that he told you not to move anything again, you heard something in his voice—anger, simple and clean—that you'd never heard before.

A guy named Allen Gump lived on Cleveland's west side and had an acquaintance named Barnes. Barnes and his minor sidekick Michael visited Gump often enough to know he owned just the help they needed to upgrade their business in a hurry without a cent of overhead. Gump owned a .38 blue-steel snub-nosed revolver. Barnes needed the gun, so he broke into his friend's house and took it.

On December 12, 1974, just about twenty-four hours before Barnes would become a murderer, he decided to step things up. Now he had a gun. All he needed was another tulip ready to be plucked.

Richard Wilkinson stopped his silver two-door 1972 Mercury XR7 at a red light near Perkins Beach. As he waited for the light to change, his passenger door flung open, and Wilkinson stared into the two-inch barrel of a .38 caliber revolver.

"Freeze or I'll shoot you, you bitch," the gunman said, his hazel eyes flashing. "If you move I'll blow your balls off with this gun."

Barnes, with his hair slicked back and greasy under a black leather cap with a brim, a green field jacket and light-colored plaid pants, forced Wilkinson to drive to Perkins Beach.

You visit Perkins Beach, take pictures, time distances to get things right. On the way home you go out of your way to drive past your aunt's house. If you see her outside, you'll stop and visit. See if she feels like talking about her dead husband. Surely a quarter of a century has eased the pain. After all, they were on their way to a divorce when he was killed, you tell yourself as you pass duplex after duplex. You see her outside. She's playing with her grandchildren in the rear of her narrow driveway. It's a beautiful summer afternoon. You keep driving.

When they arrived at Perkins, Barnes forced Wilkinson into the back seat. Barnes's accomplice sat in the passenger seat. The minor, referred to only as Michael, who stood no more than a few inches over five feet tall and weighed less than one hundred and forty pounds, wore a black sweater with blue stripes, shoulder-length brown hair parted on the left. He held the .38 Titan Tiger on Wilkinson while Barnes did the driving.

Barnes drove Michael and their victim to an apartment complex, where he stopped the car and got out to inspect the trunk. He reached into the trunk, produced a tire iron and got back in the car.

"You better come up with fifty dollars or we'll kill you," Barnes said, brandishing the weapon.

"I don't have any money," Wilkinson said.

Barnes then dragged him out of the back seat, smacked him on the head with the barrel of the gun and threw him into the trunk.

Barnes and the kid sped around enjoying the power and speed of the XR7. Every half hour or so, Barnes would pull the car over, open the trunk and crack Wilkinson in the head with the tire iron. By the time Barnes freed Wilkinson from the trunk, the young kid was gone, and Wilkinson was forced back up front.

"I really just want to be friends" Barnes said as he held the .38 on Wilkinson. "You should come and see me . . ."

After his bizarre comments about becoming friends, Barnes stopped the car in the parking lot of a dry cleaners and got out, telling Wilkinson to head west and to keep going.

Weeks before you were to make the sacrament of Confirmation at St. Bridget's Catholic Church, you asked Uncle Don if he would be your sponsor, somebody willing to stand for and with you as you became a soldier of Christ. Uncle Don said he'd love to, but that he could not. At the time he felt he was not a good Catholic. He wasn't even receiving Communion. He refused to be a hypocrite by playing the role of good soldier. He apologized for letting you down. You admired him for his honesty. You hoped you had the courage one day to follow his lead.

Just after 6 p.m. Don maneuvers his 1971 Lincoln into the entrance to Edgewater Park and moves slowly up the drive to Perkins Beach, where unbeknownst to him, Barnes waits, finishing take-out chicken and sipping a can of RC Cola.

Perhaps Don checks himself out in the rearview mirror, slips his glasses into their black case, nods in a knowing way that he looks good. Although he's still wearing his work clothes, light gray pants and matching work shirt with Houghton Elevator sewn over the right shirt pocket and his name stitched over the left, he looks fine, dapper even. His brown dress shoes ease up on the accelerator as he nears the portal to Perkins. The temperature this close to the lake is only a couple degrees above freezing; Don's lucky he wore his blue nylon work jacket.

He backs into a spot along the cul-de-sac, turns off his headlights, and then the engine. To his left and across a more inland section of the shoreline the lights of Cleveland shine through the oncoming darkness. He sees the Terminal Tower. Behind him sit leafless trees, and beyond the trees a black drop-off to the shallowest of the five Great Lakes. On the other side of the cul-de-sac stands a sixty-three-year-old statue of German composer Richard Wagner. Wagner's beret-topped head angles away from Perkins Beach; his coat looks as though it has been blown open, and he holds a sheaf of music in his left hand. Don gazes around casually, non-committally, perhaps clicking the ball point pen in his shirt pocket or fingering the yellow-handled pocketknife in his pants.

Barnes licks three chicken bones clean, throws them into the black plastic box they came in and drops the box to the ground. Another tulip. And this time Barnes is ready. He's tired of playing around.

When he sees the young man approaching his car, does Don's heart pick up speed? Does he quickly rehearse his lines, or does he know the drill? Does he check his hair one last time, frustrated by the tinges of gray growing above the ears? Does he lower his power windows a bit to convey a welcome? Is this his first time, the time he's fantasized about, the time he's been forbidden to fantasize about? Forbidden himself to fantasize about? Does his conscience tingle with the electric knowledge you get when you know something's wrong and you do it anyway, as if you're moving through everything you are and know to enter another place, whose passage you'll only worry about once you're safely back from the other side? Is this why, when Barnes pulls out his gun and demands money, Don can't possibly give it to him? Can't possibly give in to him?

Surely Don knows the fantasy is over when the minor accomplice gets in the back seat and he's forced into the passenger seat. Barnes is once again behind the wheel, still sipping his pop.

From the passenger seat Don lunges for the gun. Barnes pulls the revolver's trigger six times; two of the six hit the firing pin but do not fire. Two bullets rip through Don's right upper chest and lodge in his back. Another hits the upper left side of the neck and exits from the right side of the back. The final bullet enters in front of Don's left ear and exits through the back of the same ear. In the confusion windows are busted, blood and glass sprinkle the black vinyl roof, the seats, the maroon carpet on the floor, the door panels. While Barnes fires, Don attempts to get out the passenger side of the car. Frightened, Barnes flees, drops the gun on the front seat. Don dies before he can get away; he dies lying half in, half out of his car, his right lung perforated, specks of gun powder in the wounds, massive internal hemorrhaging, seventy-five feet away from a police call box.

The lady at the Cuyahoga County Coroner's office warns you about one of the autopsy pictures. She says you don't have to pay for that one if you don't want to. You thank her but insist on seeing all seven of them. She says okay and hands them to you, back first, so the photographs face her. "What relation was he to you?" she asks. It should be a simple question but has gotten considerably more complicated. Story to storyteller? Subject to writer? Nephew to....? "He was my uncle," you tell her. "Three and a half years ago my daughter came through here," she tells you. "That was hard." "I'm sorry," you say. "You do what you have to do, huh?" When she says this you almost think you hear her ask, "Why are you doing this?"

Around 7 p.m. on December 13, 1974, Edward Chomiak drives west on the Shoreway. Although he had hoped he could make it to his destination without having to stop, he finally decides he'll have to pull over and relieve himself. This isn't the first time he hasn't been in complete control of his body; it had betrayed him years earlier with boyhood polio.

Looking for a secluded place, Chomiak finds a darkened drive where he can relieve himself privately and be back on his way. But then he notices something. Although it is already dark and the weather's becoming more miserable, a light attracts Chomiak's attention. Walking with difficulty, he moves closer toward the light until he can make out its source, which is a dome light shining in the evening in what appears to be an abandoned car. He looks toward the middle of the cul-de-sac, to the third tree west of the center. Getting closer, he sees that the driver's side window has been smashed or the glass blown out, something. Because of his lack of agility, he heads carefully toward a Ford Falcon parked across from the Lincoln, where a man in his twenties with dark curly hair and slight beard sits alone.

"You better go call the police," Chomiak tells the curly-haired man. "I think there's a body by that car over there."

"I'll call from a gas station on Detroit. And then I'll be back," the young man says before driving away.

It's almost 7:30 now. The police have still not arrived, and the curly-haired young man has not returned. Chomiak assumes that the kid has taken off without ever calling the police, apparently not wanting to be associated with a crime at Perkins Beach.

Chomiak drives the short distance to Detroit Ave. to make the call. At 7:51 p.m. Det. Bob Shankland and Det. Jimmy Fuerst arrive. Shankland, muscular, with a reputation as a tough, brave and gutsy no-holds-barred kind of cop with reddish-brown hair, heads directly to the Lincoln, where he'll collect pop cans and soil samples. His partner, Fuerst, a fun-loving, well-liked, stocky guy gets Chomiak's story and then, noticing he's partially paralyzed, gently takes Chomiak by the arm and walks him over to the Lincoln to see if he can identify the body.

Although Chomiak remembers looking into the upturned and bloody face of the dead man, the police report it differently. The victim was found lying outside the passenger door, face down, feet together and pointing south, left arm under the body and the right arm outstretched along the right leg, head pointing north. No mention of his soul leaving his body, tumble-drifting down, above and across the lake, flying fast and safe to the far north beyond the water.

Chomiak, who still thinks of the dead man and says a prayer for him whenever he passes by this place, stares at the once-handsome now blood-smeared face of the stranger.

You take one look at the autopsy pictures. One. The woman with the dead daughter was right. You should have thought twice about acquiring the pictures. The wounds, both entrance and exit, are confirmed. Chomiak's right about the blood-smeared face. You glimpse Uncle Don through the façade of the murdered man. Yes, it's him. No, it isn't. Both equal and separate truths. You should have spent more time with the woman from the coroner's office, the one with the dead daughter. You should have listened to her tale of love and loss. You need to talk to your aunt, your deceased mother's closest sister. The time has come.

In the middle of the front seat, strewn cold, were car keys, and next to the keys, hot and spent, rested the .38 blue-steel revolver, an Arminius Titan Tiger, serial number 023805. Because Gump had reported his gun stolen, the trail led easily to Barnes. He and his minor accomplice were arrested while sitting on a couch the day after the murder. Barnes confessed immediately.

Uncle Don was taken to St. John's Hospital where he was pronounced dead at 10:05 p.m. on Friday, December 13, 1974.

My aunt asked if we would mind keeping the Lincoln at our house for a time. Perhaps she asked because my father was not only my uncle's friend but an ex-homicide detective. At first it simply took up space in our driveway and in my imagination. Soon we investigated it, my father piecing together clues, explaining to his young sons the likelihoods and probabilities: the shards of glass told one part of the story, the blood another part, the smell—in its utter indescribability—yet another. Soon we sat behind the wheel. Fearing a dead battery, my dad and I began driving the car, leaving the pieces of glass and splotches of dried blood where they lay. High school friends flocked to the car the way they were expected to. Soon the car was gone, at least from the driveway.

Good friends of my aunt and uncle—friends who lived directly across the street from them—bought the Lincoln; my uncle's then ten-year-old daughter saw it every single morning she left for school, each day she went out to play.

You call your aunt and ask her if you can visit. You ask her if she's willing to talk about Uncle Don. She says she will but that she will not do it over the phone. "He was a free spirit; that's for sure," she says. You stop at a local deli and pick up sliced turkey breast, Swiss cheese and a loaf of Italian bread, as is a family custom—not the specifics, just the gesture. Her oldest sister is also in town. They both want to talk about their parents. How one came from Italy as a twelve-year-old, about the hardships their lovely, strong and gentle mother, your grandmother, endured. You love these stories and let them lull you away from what you want to talk about. Soon they produce boxes and bags of pictures of family and its extensions.

"The guy who killed Uncle Don got released from prison in 1989," you say when a photo of Uncle Don comes up. "He served fifteen years. There wasn't even a trial. He pled to a lesser offense of murder, aggravated robbery and kidnapping."

You don't tell her that you located Barnes, that he's been living in the same house for about the last seven years. That you tried to talk to him. That he's living with at least two other men, including a chiropractor with a bad back. You don't admit that your repeated phone calls enraged a guy running interference for Barnes. 'I know Alan. I'm friends with Alan. I will talk to Alan, but if I were you I wouldn't hold my breath.' You don't tell her about the letter you wrote

100

him, asking about the murder that "rightly or wrongly" he was convicted of committing, asking about that night in December, twenty-five years ago, for information that only he can supply. You don't bother telling your aunt that the guy who killed her husband never responded to your request for information.

"That's horrible the way Don died," Aunt Manny, the elder aunt, says. "Being shot and all like that."

Uncle Don's wife is silent for a moment and it makes you want to turn and run in shame. You know at that moment that you won't be able to ask her the questions you came prepared to ask. You're sitting in her kitchen which looks exactly the way it did twenty-five years ago. You remember one Saturday night, probably thirty years ago now. Your aunt and uncle sit with your parents playing Pinochle in this very kitchen. Hand after hand. Cigarette after cigarette. Drink after drink. Laughter. Friendship. You're in the living room watching "Mannix." Never before or since have you felt so simply loved, so perfectly safe. Your aunt's a good woman and an even better aunt. She's your godmother. And in a generation and a religion that took godparenting seriously, she took it more seriously than most.

"Here's some pictures of Don," she says.

You take up one of him in tennis whites standing next to a Cadillac. Another where he's lounging on an army cot during the service; he's wearing his uniform and a huge smile. You wonder how many points of view it takes to tell anything about anybody.

"This is your grandpa," my aunt says to her oldest grandchild, whom she babysits a couple of days a week.

The boy, holding a stack of baseball cards in his fist, stops for a second and looks at the black-and-white picture. Of course, the statement is as true as it is false. There is no doubt that the blood of the man is coursing through the body of the boy. Yes, that's his grandfather. No, it isn't the whole picture.

What do you do with all the circumstantial evidence? All the other pictures? All the rumors about the guys Uncle Don moved in with after he left his wife. A family member asking him, 'Why are you hanging out with these queers?' Uncle Don's response, 'Don't knock it if you haven't tried it.' And what about Perkins Beach? What about the tulip vultures? What about going miles out of his way on a miserable evening to sit in a dark park with a reputation as a homosexual hangout? What about the other strangers? Did he die because he couldn't live as an openly gay man? Would there have been less pressure if he had lived anywhere but Lakewood, anywhere other than "gay city"? Was his death ultimately caused by force, threat or deception? All three? Threats from whom? Who was deceived?

But who's the real person? How vain and egomaniacal is it to think you know? How foolish? How wrongheaded? Does loving somebody and being a writer give you a right to his story? You cannot tell your aunt what you've learned, and you hope she never reads this story.

In one photograph Uncle Don and Aunt Dee stand in front of the fireplace in their Christmas-tree lit living room in the early 1960s, not long after their wedding. Flowers adorn the wooden mantel, as do a bronze plate and a candle. Two snowmen stand sentry, flanking the flower arrangement. Two Christmas stockings—a few years away from being three—hang from the mantel. In the background, in front of a window covered with a soft, white cotton curtain, a saint with a crown of gold and a gown of white stands atop a corner cupboard with glass doors. Small, light blue designs decorate Uncle Don's white, short-sleeve shirt. He wears navy blue slacks with a thin black belt. Aunt Dee's green dress curves perfectly with her form; there's a gold pin above her left breast.

Uncle Don's arms are wrapped around his wife's waist. Her right hand holds his left wrist. My aunt's smile at his holding makes her beautiful. Uncle Don's smile rules and lines his face.

Their smiles appear to be evidence of something. Of something good. Something worth telling. They seem, at this captured moment in time, two people possessed of all the love that can possibly exist in a world where people are murdered.

When You Write about Murder

When you write about murder it's best to start with a few facts. The first one is this: The man killed was somebody's father and husband and friend and uncle. Fact number two: So too was the guy who killed him.

When you write about murder, begin with police reports. Police reports, while not artfully written, can tell you all kinds of revealing things. They can tell you that your uncle's body was found seventy-five feet away from a police call box. They can tell you that the killer used a .38 blue-steel revolver, an Arminius Titan Tiger, serial number 023805. From police reports you can learn what the victim was wearing and what he had in his pockets.

When you write about murder, even if the murder happened over twenty-five years ago, be sure to accompany your dad, an ex-homicide detective, when he goes to inspect your uncle's car, a 1971 maroon Lincoln Continental. Pay attention when your dad's explaining to his then sixteen-year-old son—just by looking at the car—how it must have happened. "One guy in the passenger seat, another in back. The guy in the passenger seat fired the gun." Pay attention when he explains glass and blood splatter. If you can, turn your head away from the car every minute or so. Breathe in the cold outside air. Try as hard as you can to ignore the hair splattered on the driver's side and stuck on the head rest. Don't worry about the stench. No matter how many times you try, you'll never be able to describe it to anybody.

When you write about murder, regardless of how many scenes you visit or police reports you read or cops or witnesses you interview, you'll never be able to fathom why good friends of your aunt and uncle—friends who lived directly across the street from them—bought the Lincoln, forcing your uncle's then ten-year-old daughter to have to see it every morning she left for school, each day she went out to play. When you write about murder, understand that why the guy killed your uncle is the easier question to answer. Why his friends bought the car he was murdered in will remain forever inexplicable.

When you write about murder—say the murder of a family member—always be sure to justify yourself within the text. Never pretend you're justifying it to yourself because you don't have to, but not everybody will understand. Say something like this: "Somehow I always knew much of what happened to my uncle had become a family fiction. Maybe it was the way the story never changed, as if one detail out of place would cause the entire narrative edifice to come tumbling down, resembling a collapsed cathedral, its glory betrayed by the sudden clutter of its bricks. For whatever reason I have remained selfishly, seriously curious for over twenty-five years. I know I loved him, and I'm hoping this love is enough to attempt to tell his story." When you write about murder, ask yourself if love ever has a thing to do with any of it.

When you write about murder, don't be too excited when your reporting reveals what you had suspected. It's unseemly. It's beneath you. As you ride down the elevator in the Justice Center in Cleveland, try hard to hide your glee—yes, your fucking glee—upon learning that at the time your uncle was murdered other men also claiming not to be gay were robbed and beaten at Edgewater Park. It seems some kids were preying on closeted gay men, luring them down to the lake's edge with the promise of sex, and then robbing them. It was a good scam, until the kids went too far and killed somebody who put up a fight.

When you write about murder ignore your uncle's marriage to your aunt, how it must have been for her after the separation; what it must have been like for him before.

When you write about murder, pay heed to the woman at the coroner's office who warns you about one of the autopsy pictures. She says you don't have to pay for the one if you don't want to. You thank her but insist on seeing all seven. She says ok and hands them to you, back first, so the photographs face her. "What relation was he to you?" she asks. It should be a simple question but has gotten considerably more complicated. Story to storyteller? Subject to writer? Nephew to...? He was my uncle, you tell her. "Three and a half years ago my daughter came through here," she tells you. "That was hard." "I'm sorry," you say. "You do what you have to do, huh"? When she says this you almost think you hear her ask, 'Why are you doing this?'

When you write about murder, for Christ's sake, stop what you're doing long enough to ask a helpful woman about her murdered daughter. The story will wait. Your soul is in peril.

When you write about murder work hard to get the details right and the right details. Drive a 1971 Lincoln Continental. Hold a .38 blue-steel revolver, an Arminius Titan Tiger. Visit Edgewater Park at 6 p.m. on Friday the 13th, December, the exact date twenty-five years after the murder. Be sure to remember how much has changed. A tree grows a lot in that time. So don't assume anything. Get pictures of the time and place and study them for clues of the way things were, whether the murder was last month or long ago. Check with the weather bureau so you have right weather on the right day.

When you write about murder, never forget you're writing about human beings, and never forget you must transform them into characters. People who had one precious life, just like you, and then that life was gone. Remember that the whole life was not defined by a murder—only ended by one. Do months of reporting and researching and soul-searching and rationalizing and then give it your best shot. When you write about murder, do not make up a single thing. Remember: this is somebody's father or husband or Uncle Don.

"On the night of the murder, Don maneuvers his 1971 Lincoln into the entrance to Edgewater Park and moves slowly up the drive to Perkins Beach, where, unbeknownst to him, a guy named Barnes waits, finishing take out chicken, and sipping a can of R.C. Cola.

When he sees the young man approaching his car, does Don's heart pick up speed? ... Is this the first time, the first time he's fantasized about, the time he's forbidden himself to fantasize about? Does his conscience tingle with the electric knowledge you get when you know something's wrong and you do it anyway, as if you're moving through everything you are and know to enter another place, whose passage you'll only worry about once you're safely back on the other side? Is this why, when the killer destroys the fantasy by pulling out his gun and demanding money, Don can't possibly give it to him? Can't possibly give in to him?"

When you write about murder, it is here you'll write about four bullets entering a body and killing a man, somebody's father, son, husband, uncle.

When you write about murder and then wonder why you did, find an old photograph from Christmastime, 1960 something. Stare at Uncle Don and Aunt Dee standing in front of their wooden mantel. Two Christmas stockings—still a few years away from being three—hang behind them. In the background, in front of a window covered with soft, white, cotton curtains, a saint with a crown of gold and a gown of white stands atop a corner cupboard with glass doors.

Uncle Don's arms are wrapped around his wife's waist. Her right hand holds his left wrist. Your aunt's smile at his holding makes her beautiful. Uncle Don's smile rules and lines his face. Their smiles appear to be evidence of something, true evidence. Of something good. Of a story worth telling. They seem, at this captured moment in time, two people possessed of all the love that can possibly exist in a world where people are murdered, and where other people presume to write about it.

Stop-time #6

In the spring of 1786, Abraham Lincoln—namesake and grandfather of our 16th president—was planting corn on his rural Kentucky homestead with the help of his three boys, Mordecai, Josiah, and Thomas, the youngest. A small party of what most accounts believe to be Shawnee attacked the four Lincolns, killing Abraham and scattering the boys to a nearby cabin, all except eight-year-old Thomas who stayed put, standing by his father's body. One of the Shawnee braves grabbed Thomas, holding him against his chest and running off into the woods. Mordecai, the oldest son at fourteen, picked up a rifle, fired through a gap in the logs of the cabin, killing the Shawnee and saving the life of Thomas. If Thomas had been killed or taken to live with the Native Americans, there would be no Thomas Lincoln and no son, Abraham Lincoln. Without President Abraham Lincoln, what else would have been lost?

Gazing at My Father Gazing

From across the lake I live on, I gaze at my father's house, the white rails rimming the porch, the age-stained stone steps saved from the razed ruins of his boyhood school. I can see his canoe and kayaks, empty. As I stand here, trying to remain in the moment, I mourn the loss of my father, although he is alive and well.

A few things to know about my father: He's worked as a bricklayer and served a stint in the Air Force during the Korean War. He walked the streets of Cleveland dressed as a woman. Not for the sheer thrill of it, which is what I'd assumed, but while he was employed as a detective on the intelligence unit of the Cleveland Police force. Because there weren't any female police officers on the streets in the late fifties, early sixties and because my dad was skinny and fair, he'd been elected to work on what was then called the decoy squad, where he seductively ambled up and down the city streets, hoping to be mugged, in which case he'd radio a partner and make an arrest on perp or perv. Once at a bachelor party for a mutual friend, the nephew of one of my dad's old partners approached me after a few drinks. He told me he saw a picture of my dad undercover, and then he said the words I'll remember forever: "Your dad was not a bad looking woman." These words filled me, in equal measure, with an immense terror and a prurient pride.

Right now my father's likely checking on the killdeer mother who has made his home her nest, laying her light-blue speckled eggs in gravel, rubbing her chest on the ground, displacing the stones and forming a smooth, camouflaged space where she deposits her offspring. The species is famous for the female's wounded wing act, which she performs whenever she feels her nest is in danger. She screeches, scurrying away, one wing flat against her side, the other out like a sail, attempting to divert a potential predator's attention. This urgent instinct to protect her young has forced my father to change his habits, which at his age are pretty firmly entrenched. Because the killdeer deposited her eggs smack in the middle of his driveway, my dad has parked near the road instead of near his house, which has been his custom. While most of his front grass is shorn to a respectable length, he's kept his lawnmower a decent distance from the nest, which has created a square of grass the size of a shed and the height of a mid-July cornfield. Having ordered a ton of gravel he'd planned to distribute around his back porch, my father had originally figured to guide the delivery dump truck up his driveway, making sure the bird's unhatched young stayed safe between the truck's wheels. But when the load arrived, he abandoned his plan. He instead instructed the driver to dump the full ton of stone at the edge of the driveway, afraid not doing so would inadvertently send the killdeer mother into paroxysms of anxiety. My eighty-four-year-old father, who suffered three heart attacks in middle age, then shoveled and hauled the ton of gravel to the back of his house, wheelbarrow load after wheelbarrow load, resulting in no extra stress on the killdeer, just aches in the well-worn muscles of one old man.

Before and after his turn as not a bad looking woman, he worked first in a patrol car and then ended his ten-year career as a homicide detective. He even rode in the back of a paddy wagon with the Beatles, safely escorting the lads from their hotel to the music hall for the band's first Cleveland concert. After leaving the police force after ten years, my dad started a street-cleaning business, which was successful until it wasn't. Not long after his business failed and in grave debt, refusing on principle to declare bankruptcy, he returned to police work, only this time as a cop in a small town. He quit the day he had to put down a rabid dog. He also worked for a time as a private detective, which I loved, especially accompanying him on stakeouts, sleuthing to discover the titillating—for a twelve-year-old boy— evidence of marital infidelity. When my mother fell ill with cancer, my dad got a job at a Cleveland steel mill, laying brick in blast furnaces. He hated the job above all else, but he stuck it out because with my mother sick we needed the health insurance. Around this time, he also studied with an Amish man because he wanted to learn how to make oak and hickory Amish rocking chairs. Soon he had a shop set up in our garage complete with a furnace and steamer and molds for shaping rocking chair arms and legs. He built and sold these rockers and later Adirondack chairs.

In his sixties, he bought a used sailboat, taught himself to be its captain and ended up routinely sailing from the islands of Lake Erie to the waters of Canada. When he turned eighty-two, he called me and said, "Let's buy kayaks," although he'd never sat in one in his life. He now owns two. Just a month before he turned eighty-four, he adopted a black lab puppy, who's morphed into a giant of a dog who, albeit accidentally and lovingly, has knocked him to the ground more than once. My youngest sister believes we should impose a delay on any new idea our father voices, something resembling the waiting period for buying an assault rifle.

Soon all my family on the lake, four generations of us now that my daughter, her husband and two of our four granddaughters also live here, eagerly await the killdeer births. We tread carefully when we visit. My young granddaughters lie down a few feet away and stare, eyes level with the invisible umbilicus between mother and young, creating names for the four soon-to-be-baby birds. In the nesting's second week, my dad tied a trail camera to a nearby tree in order to chronicle the birth. He bought the camera originally to record the famed first jump of baby wood ducks. Last winter he suddenly decided we needed to build a wood duck house, so we did. He researched the specifications for the perfect wood duck home, complete with the size of the box itself, dimensions of the hole, depth of wood chips for a bed, and even a scrim of screen on the inside beneath the portal which would allow the babies to scamper up their Mackall-made home and out into the world. After the house's completion, we affixed the camera to a nearby tree, hoping to catch sight of the ducks. Although we never thought we'd actually get the ducks to choose our home as theirs, they did. When wood duck babies are born the mother leaves a house or a hole in a tall tree, and her weightless ducklings drift to the ground or the water to follow her, whether they're seven feet up or seventy. Unfortunately, the motion-activated trail camera we bought was not sensitive or sophisticated enough to capture the virgin voyage of the wood duck young. But we assumed it would work on the killdeer.

I've learned a lot about myself, my dad and the passing of time in the four years since his second wife's death. He likes to say he's the only person he knows who's been happily married twice, to my mother for twenty-two years, and then to my mother's best friend for thirty-two. The problem with being happily married twice in my father's case is that he's buried both wives.

Having four generations of us living in the same place has only heightened my ever-increasing and nearly debilitating angst over something as natural and primeval as the passing of time. I'll awake at three in the morning to pee and get distracted by photos of my family scrolling benignly across my wife's computer screen. My granddaughters smile in every picture, blissfully beautiful and dangerously innocent. Since having granddaughters nine years ago, I've been overtaken by time's skeletal grip. Time has collapsed. Past, present and future exist simultaneously and uncomfortably. On television there's live breaking news on one channel and a Western I watched as a child on another. We take pictures on our phones of seemingly every other moment as it occurs, the present becoming the past in a millisecond, archived for a digital future we may not live to see. Teasing time apart at times is impossible. Fear over this fills me. I exist in the past and present one minute, solely the past the next. And at times, like when I wallow in a dark hole in deep night, I stare masochistically into the futures of my children and grandchildren, where I see mushroom clouds and super viruses, a vanquished America, a white-hot vanishing planet.

Sometimes I gaze into a photo from a past before I was born and see how much of time's passing it reveals, how much of the future it foretells. I'm thinking of a picture of my father and mother posing with their wedding party hours after my parents consecrated their marriage in St. Thomas's Catholic Church in Cleveland. Last fall my father handed me the wedding picture asking if I could make a copy of it, removing everybody except himself, my mother and my mother's best friend. In the photo he stands between his two wives. It's instructive to consider the story the photo tells now and the one it foretold sixty years ago. Dad's holding my mom's hand; his other hand rests on a wooden folding chair that makes it appear as though he's holding his future wife's hand as well. But he's not. Their time will come. First there will be four children and school and work and Christmases and summers—nothing more or less really than the excruciatingly ordinary passing of time—and then will arrive cancer and death and things happening that those two newlyweds could not have imagined on that effervescent October afternoon. Because of poor photography, my mother's white wedding gown merges with the white walls behind her, foreshadowing her oncoming absence. The visible white of my dad's shirt, the section covering his heart, makes it appear as though a part of him will disappear as well. Whoever took the photo also happened to catch a woman from the kitchen in the background, just behind and to the left of my dad and his two wives. I asked my father if he wanted me to crop out the woman from the kitchen. "What woman?" he asked.

Day after day for more than three weeks we grew increasingly obsessed with the killdeer and her young. "Anything new with the killdeer?" one of us would ask. "She's still sitting there," my father would answer. I must admit to once or twice approaching what I knew would be too close to the mother bird, just so my granddaughters could glimpse the eggs. This is the kind of shit that happens to you when you live too long in the country. (I'll also admit to listening to the lake's ice cracking in winter, which is truly a haunting and lovely sound.) It's easy to make fun of it. I do it too. With everything going on in the world, what weight does the birth of a few killdeers carry? Who knows? Not much, I guess, but my dad, despite pain and loss and dwindling days, is always and ever on the side of life.

I'm troubled by my father's ability to always move forward. I'm not sure I could live with losing my beloved and loving wife, who has a bad heart and chronic asthma. As my brother said to me once: "If something ever happened to Dandi, you'd be living in a fucking cardboard box on the street." I couldn't argue with him.

When I first heard the cliché that old age isn't for sissies—somebody else's word, not mine—sometime in my twenties, I was dismissive. What the hell does that have to do with me? Now when I hear it I, naturally, drown in dread. That's really all I got. I'm a total wimp. It's who I am. I know this as certainly as I know I'm white and bald and straight. Although my father wrestled in high school, boxed in the Air Force and was an accomplished swimmer, he's not a macho man, and neither are his sons. He never watched sports or hung out with the guys as did most of the men in our factory-fueled, working-class neighborhood. His tenderness is deep and his capacity for love is wide, but he is tough; meaning, I suppose, that he simply does what he has to do.

I hate this about him.

Two years ago he stood over his toilet urinating blood, only telling me about it days later. "Why didn't you call me or an ambulance or go to the emergency room?" I asked. He said that if it kept happening, he'd call his doctor. When my brother heard the news, he called me from his home in LA. "Wouldn't you go to the hospital if you were pissing blood?" he asked. "The second I regained consciousness," I replied. My brother and I bemoan the fact that we're shadows of our father. "We're both total pussies," one of us will say to the other, needlessly affirming what we both already know.

When I had to have my gums numbed for a deep cleaning of my teeth recently, I called my younger brother, asking him to help watch over my family if the teeth cleaning went south. He assured me he would.

After an operation more than a decade ago, my dad was forced to use a catheter twice a day for three agonizing years, which was excruciatingly painful and psychologically difficult—for me and my brother. Even as I write this, beads of sweat bubble up on my forehead. And likely my brother's as well, although he's two thousand miles away. Because this we know we could not do.

The walls of the lakefront home my father built are covered with pictures of his parents and grandparents, aunts and uncles, wives and brothers, ancestors near and distant who lived lives of nearly unimaginable hardship, having to endure events I know I could not survive.

I look at a picture of my father's father who was pulled out of school when he was twelve to work in the western Pennsylvania coal mines.

I see my father's grandfather who had to drop out of school at nine to work in the western Pennsylvania coal mines.

I imagine his uncle who died of black lung in his forties after having worked the western Pennsylvania coal mines.

I watch a distant cousin I know only through story, skipping around her house at age five in a new dress on the morning the hem catches the flames from the gas stove.

I look at the aunt who drowned in drink for the rest of her life because her daughter burned to death at age five.

The aunt who buried three children.

The father-in-law who buried his one-year-old daughter.

The father-in-law who was fired from his job during the Great Depression the same week he buried his one-year-old daughter.

And on it goes.

So it often seems as though more than four generations reside on our lake together. These ancestors come to life in the stories my father tells. His way of keeping them alive in the imagination of his oldest child, I suppose. Ancestors enter times they would never live to see. I believe he's passing them on to me in story before he too departs this life.

Nearly every time my dad and I make the five-mile walk around the lake, our mother accompanies us, although she's been dead for nearly forty years. "Your mother would have loved having grandchildren," he'll say. "She would have been so proud of everybody." Other times it's somebody else. He recently told me the story of the night his mother died, not even two months after my mother's death. Although my father came from a loving home, the love remained unstated. Nobody mouthed the words. "That night I wanted to tell my mom I loved her," he said to me, "but I didn't want to scare her. I thought if I said it, she'd be afraid she was going to die." He didn't tell her. She died that night.

It's always on our walks or kayak rides that he opens up with these storied surprises. Drifting in his kayak my dad will say things like: "Let's go to Turtle Cove and see if the wood ducks are hanging around." "I wonder if I'll see another summer." "I watched a mother duck with five ducklings one morning and four the next, I want to see if we can find the other one." "I wouldn't have a problem with death if everybody always went in order." "Did you see the moon last night?" "Did you hear the cry of the loon the other evening?" "I hope we see the kingfisher this summer." "Your mom would have loved it here."

One morning walk last summer, he stunned me still. My dad, who, like me, grew up Catholic (although he was the product of a marriage between a Catholic and a Protestant) professes to believe next to nothing now. He's never found succor or solace in Catholicism. He hated the numberless and seemingly insurmountable and arbitrary rules of the faith, and he's turned off by dogma, as well as preaching from anybody about anything. When the Catholic cemetery holding the remains of our family dead refused to bury my Protestant grandfather, my father was finished with the church, and I think, religious faith of any stripe. But on the walk around the lake last summer, he told me he'd decided to attempt belief in an afterlife. He figured he'd be happier if he did believe, things would be easier, and that he just couldn't stand the idea of never seeing Peg, his second wife, again. Although I didn't ask about his wanting to see her, I assumed my father had long ago resigned himself to never again laying eyes on my mother.

Finally, one day the killdeer and her eggs are gone. Everybody wonders why not a single piece of shell remains. We then learn that a mother will often carry away the shells and drop them far from the hatching place. My dad and my granddaughters are excited to find out if the trail camera captured the birth, the eggs cracking open, tiny wet heads squirming out, the wobbly first steps. I remove the memory card from the camera, stick it in my dad's laptop and scan the pictures for the birth. Even without the images, the story of the killdeer and her young is set in the minds of four generations of us. A story received and offered up by a century of people achieves its own truth. 'Remember when the killdeer had babies in Pap Pap's driveway, the way he tried not to freak out the mother, carrying tons of gravel in a wheelbarrow for hours in the scorching afternoon sun?' And we'll go silent and remember the man who's no longer alive. We'll smile melancholy smiles and tell other stories. We don't really need to see the images, not if we have the story.

So I tell my granddaughters the bad news. "It was a cheap camera. We'll get a better one next year."

Not long after the storied birth of the killdeers, I confess to my father what I could not reveal to my granddaughters. Even with trying everything in our power to protect this mother bird and her young, day after day for more than three weeks, neither the mother nor we could save the babies. As I flicked through the images, I saw the stalking night silhouette of a fox appearing out of a gray stillness. In one moment the mother's on her eggs. In the next a deadly blur, the fox not fooled by the mother's act. In the next frame, after having devoured the eggs, the fox is gone. Past, present and future in an instant. Four incubated and worried-over lives gone before they arrived, consumed by another wild creature interested only and ever in staying alive.

My father embarked on his final career after my mother died, which was building and selling houses in a small lake development in rural Ohio. Although this dream didn't work out quite the way he'd planned, it became something far greater than he could have imagined.

Of the four houses my dad built on the lake, strangers live in just two of them. He lives in a beautiful little brick house right on the lake; my children grew up in another, the house I live in now. In a house my dad did not build but is no more than two minutes away from him and only ten from me, my daughter lives with her husband and two of my granddaughters. So although nobody would have seen this as the outcome of a desperate move my father made after losing his first wife, this lake is home. My dad calls this accidental place our mother's posthumous bequest to her family, even the two generations she didn't live long enough to know.

My fear is that I won't be able to take over when my father dies. I'm not tough enough. I don't believe I have what it takes. Perhaps my heart isn't big enough. I don't thrill to the tiniest life forms the way my father does. I don't gaze upon every dawn and deem it beautiful. I spend too much time fighting cynicism and ennui. And yet, and yet, I do love, even if I love like a lunatic: desperate and messy and fiercely and wild. Love allows me to swim daily in the waters of what's possible. Maybe I have a shot. I do tell stories; that we share.

And for the time being, I can gaze at my father's house across the lake, the white rails rimming the porch, the age-stained stone steps saved from the razed ruins of his boyhood school, where I see him pulling out the kayaks for our ride on which I learn to listen for the call of the loon, long for the birth of ducklings in spring, eye the diving buffleheads in fall, all the while feeling the rhythmic wash of the waves as we paddle on, dipping our fingers in fresh water, gazing into the storied, blinding lushness of now.

Stop-time #7

In 1856, not long after he returned home from doing "God's work" at the home of settlers who lived along Pottawattamie Creek in Kansas, John Brown received a letter from his daughter, Ruth, and in the letter, she relates a message from Brown's grandson. Ruth writes: "Johnny says, 'Tell Grandfather that I hope he will live to come back here again.'" Here's Brown's grandson eager to see his grandfather. And even if Brown was carrying out the work of God as he contends, he and seven followers butchered five people believed to have been slaveholders, an incident that became known as the Pottawattamie Massacre. I'm not sure why, but I've always imagined Brown reading this letter with the blood of his victims deep in the folds of his skin, as if he were born that way. I picture him leaning back in a chair at his kitchen table in the blurry orbital glow of a kerosene lamp or creaking in a rocking chair on his porch as dusk dawns, smudging the pages of the letter with the blood that would not wash off for days, and Brown smiling, reading of his grandson's desire to see his grandpa.

Fighting Flight

Lately I've been haunted by birds. Not in an Alfred Hitchcock/Tippy Hedren kind of way. It's more insidious and subtle than that. For most of my life I've never really liked or trusted birds. They were too abundant, too dirty, too confident, catching the thermals of their dinosaur descendancy. And now they infiltrate each square foot of my yard, making nests on nearly every windowsill, dormer and downspout, chirping innocently, singing pretty songs, downing passenger planes. Although I've always been fascinated with eagles and falcons and hawks, birds with the violent integrity of predators, and I'll also admit to having a soft spot for certain ducks and even the ubiquitous geese, honking and shitting their way over and through every subdivision in America, the small yard birds never captured my imagination or even much of my attention. (I must confess here that while listening to geese honking overhead in the darkening dead of winter while I'm hauling firewood through drifts of snow, spotting my wife through the window in the yellow light of our kitchen, I often get a spinal chill that can only be called a haunting, making me acutely aware of the brutal coexistence of beauty and oblivion.)

But somehow the older I get, it's these small, everyday birds I'm troubled by: sparrows and titmice and chickadees and robins and cardinals and blue jays and swallows and red-winged black birds and grackles and purple martins. For my entire youth and for much of my adult life, I've simply never cared for any of them. Perhaps it's more accurate to say that I never gave them much thought. I didn't like or dislike them. They were simply part of my world, the way of factory smoke and no fish on Fridays.

Recently however, something has changed, which I blame on becoming a grandfather nine years ago this summer. If I spot a cardinal alighting on a blue spruce whose branches are covered in snow, my breath catches in my throat. A moment of awe ensues. I park my car at the end of my driveway, so I don't disturb the feeding of a pileated woodpecker. In the right mood I'll struggle to stave off melancholy at the mourning dove's achingly soft wail. I've noticed that mourning doves bother no other bird at our feeders. In fact, they stay on the ground and eat what the others discard, taking off at the slightest hint of danger or conflict, capturing the pacifism of winged grief. And all of this attention and concern I have over these birds worries me.

I'm frightened frankly because every third elderly person I know seems obsessed with birds and bird houses and bird feeders and "keeping those darn squirrels away from the bird seed." Does my interest in these birds mean that I'm already old? Perhaps it's simply their aesthetic appeal. Many are beautiful. But their beauty alone is not what's pulling me. Hell, I'm only fifty-eight. Shouldn't I be incontinent before I hang suet on branches in hopes of attracting redheaded woodpeckers? My dad is nearly eighty-six and has a wood duck house affixed to his poplar tree on our lake, as well as four bluebird houses in his front yard. That makes sense to me. I should confess here that he and I built nine bluebird houses, just so everyone in the family—even those under ninety-five and in full control of their functions—could have one of their very own. "What's a bluebird house?" my son asked when I offered him one. "A house for bluebirds, for chrissake," I answered, in a way that made me sound a hundred and ten years old. My retort sounded, in fact, haughty and a little aggrieved. Although my son and I are extremely close—he often remarks that we have a better relationship than ninety-five percent of his friends and their fathers, (I don't dare ask about the other five percent)—I thought I detected something in his question other than a quest for knowledge. I was sure he was rubbing his youth in my face. "Ha," he seemed to be saying, "I'm too virile and busy and productive and virile and have way too much of an actual life to know anything about bluebirds or their damn houses." The ancient leathery man inside me was about to remind him that it was I, young, virile man, who *brought him into this world* thirty-four years ago, but I recalled the time I used that cliché when in the midst of disciplining him when he was around twelve. It didn't have the desired effect. "Don't remind me that you had sex with my mother," he said. So I decided to leave the whole bluebird house thing alone.

Without my being initially aware, it now seems that I somehow have become personally responsible for the health and wellbeing of every bird I see. And this is thanks in large part to my two oldest granddaughters, Ellie and Cassie. It started with my dad and me being forced to dig holes and sink four by fours in both front and back yards, mounting a red feeder in front and a green in back. Now we go through about eighty pounds of birdseed every week in the front feeder alone. Birds eat about two percent of this. The rest is a diurnal Thanksgiving for all red, gray and black squirrels in the neighborhood. Every bird feeder I've ever seen boasts of being squirrel proof, of course, but these tiny terrorists know how to get around such claims. Squirrels squirm and writhe beneath the bar designed to buckle under their weight, draping themselves through the metal of the feeder as if suspended in an embrace, making it appear as though they're not merely gorging themselves on my birdseed but are in fact engaged in a full-blown sexual relationship with the feeder itself.

My shifting relationship to birds and other small creatures is not the only sign of ageing. Just the other day my wife Dandi and I sat watching a movie where two twenty-somethings were naked as jay birds—birds again?—in the throes of fresh sex, and I heard myself say: "What a magnificent chest—of drawers." Yes, I was transfixed by the elegant contours and fine craftsmanship of an antique wood dresser in the background of the lovemaking. Dandi turned her head toward me with a look on her face that seemed to be reading the "do not resuscitate" order stamped on my forehead. I'll defend myself here by citing how many movies I've seen in my fifty-eight years and in how many of those have beautiful people writhed young and firm and nude on a bed. Thousands upon thousands probably. But in contrast, how many truly gorgeous antique dressers have I beheld? Have any of us beheld?

I'm not saying I no longer seek the pleasures of the flesh. I'm still breathing after all. It's just that becoming a grandfather seems to have caused some seismic shift in me. I'm suddenly worried about everything. I feel I must care for all animals exotic, wild or domestic, particularly the small and the innocent, the vulnerable creatures my two oldest granddaughters love. Ellie and Cassie let ants crawl up their arms. Once at a cookout I spied Ellie, then around seven, lying on her stomach in the grass. Thinking she was hurt or ill, I ran over to her. "Be careful, Pa," she said to me. "I'm trying to get a cricket to jump on my arm." Last summer I had to catch and release hundreds of cicadas in their inglorious husks and incessant cries for a mate. I can't keep up with my grandchildren's desire to protect all living creatures, particularly baby birds in eggs and kittens of any stripe. Even fictional kittens.

Sometimes the girls cajole Dandi and me into playing a game they call "bad person." In this game, I'm always the bad person. Always. The rules of the game are pretty simple. The bad person, I mean, *I* adopt two kittens, and then I neglect them horribly until they sicken and must be Medevac'd to the veterinarian. The good vet, a goddess of a vet really, played by Dandi, of course, immediately soothes their ills, bestowing on them love and medicine—minus any shots—and asking questions of me, the bad person. They go like this: "Why are they so thirsty?" she'll ask. And I'll answer, "Well it hasn't rained lately. They drink out of rain puddles. If it rains, they drink." She'll ask, usually at the behest of my granddaughter kittens, "Why are they so skinny? I can see their ribs." "They have to do a better job catching rats and mice. You don't expect me to buy cat food and feed them, do you?" At this point the vet pulls the two kittens onto her lap and hugs them, and the three of them lean away from me, all the while eyeing me with contempt. At times, they even hiss. "Ask him why our fur is all torn off," Ellie will tell the vet. The vet repeats the question and I'll have to come up with a heartless reason for the furless kittens, something like, "Well, I've told them to stay away from the table saw when I'm working." "Ask him why our teeth are falling out?" Cassie commands. "It's good for them to gnaw on the steel teeth of my grizzly bear trap," I'll answer. Anyway, this game goes on and on until I'm so overwhelmed with self-loathing and my own imagined cruelty, I'll have to end it. "Let's play 'Go Fish' or 'Trouble' or have a game of catch. I can't take it anymore," I'll say to the girls. "What if when you're older you confuse me with the bad person? What if you remember me that way?" I realize I'm not kidding. I fear being conflated with the sociopath I play so well.

"We won't, Pa," Ellie will say, in a way that makes my stupid comment sound even more stupid. And then one day after an endless and brutal game of bad person when I'm sure I must have confessed to throwing my adopted kittens off a building or into a woodchipper,

Cassie, the younger of the two, says to me, "I know your real name, Pa. You're Joe Mackall."

The words hit me hard. At that moment the truth of my life descended on me with a clarity so shockingly bright, I had to turn away. Pa—the name I love and am called by only four people on earth—is a far better person than that other man. That bad person. That Joe Mackall, whoever he is.

It's hard not to wonder how we'll be viewed by our grandchildren when they become adults. Will I be forgiven my many imperfections? My crimes of passion, my sins of omission and commission? Or will I be judged solely on what kind of grandfather I've been. How have I judged my grandparents? I grew up spellbound by my maternal grandfather's story. He immigrated to the United States from Italy as a twelve-year-old boy, alone on the ship and then abandoned and alone in New York City because the uncle he was supposed to meet had returned to Italy. My grandfather never saw his parents or siblings again. Authorities pushed him through Ellis Island and onto the streets of New York. We'd always been told that an older Italian man named Frankie, a fellow immigrant from my grandpa's town of Reggio Calabria, at the toe of the boot, took him in. Frankie helped my grandfather get a job, introduced him to the Italian enclave in Brooklyn's Five Points area. My grandfather worked for Frankie at his club called the Harvard Inn on Coney Island. He started by cleaning spittoons and then worked his way up. That's a great story, I always thought. An American story. Only when I got older did I learn the truth about Frankie Yale, a Brooklyn gangster, accused of having murdered more than a few people. Yale, also a bootlegger during Prohibition, appears in every book on Al Capone, his one-time employee. And Yale was not some older man but was in fact a year younger than my grandfather, although Yale had been in the country for three years prior longer. We were told my grandfather shot himself in the leg somehow, and that while he was laid up after the "accident," Yale visited the house and offered a fifty-dollar bill to my grandmother. "Frankie, no," she said, pushing the bill back. After Yale got up from the kitchen table and left the room, my grandmother found the bill beneath his plate. She kept it. Not long after that, Capone and Johnny Torrio summoned Yale to Chicago to assassinate Big Jim Colosimo. Yale complied.

I don't know how involved my grandfather was in Yale's criminal operation or the stolen booze, but I know he was frightened enough to flee the city and start a new life. I do know I don't judge him for what he had to do to negotiate a new country, a new century. For me it's more personal than that. The thing that has always troubled me is the time when they were first married, her seventeen, pretty red-headed Irish girl from a troubled family, him twenty, when he slapped his wife, my grandmother, in the face. My grandmother told me this story. "And I told him, I said 'Leo, don't ever do that again or I'll leave.' And he never did it again, Joey, not ever." They were married for seventy-two years. It's not the hijacked booze, or Frankie Yale, or the crime or the gunshots I hear now through the miasma of memory and history. It's his hitting my grandmother that stings to this day, even though I loved my grandfather, even though he's been dead for over thirty years. How much can we count on love as the great forgiveness?

I wonder if I'll be judged by my grandchildren and for what. Cassie and Ellie are both already committed and vocal conservationists. They can't believe we've let a single species disappear. They've told me of koala bears being killed because of loss of habitat in parts of Australia. "People have to quit building so much," Ellie will say, which is usually followed by all of us watching endless YouTube videos and documentaries about the dwindling number of koalas. Cassie's obsessed with baby cheetahs. For a while she carried around a baby cheetah stuffy, pronouncing that no one be allowed to hunt cheetahs ever again. What's a grandfather to do? Dandi and I have donated money to the World Wildlife Federation, in the presence and on the urging of the girls. We also "own" a dolphin somewhere, and a couple of wolves. I want to tell them that one or two people can't bear the responsibility for the world's mishandling of the earth, but it doesn't sound quite true.

All I want to do now is repair my dormers and destroy a bird's nest. Black birds have knocked in small panels of the siding at the top of our two dormers and made nests. My brown metal roof is white with what looks like millennia of their shit. Birds come and go at all hours as if involved in a frat house ritual of procreation and destruction. I want them gone. They're nothing more than squatters. I have birdhouses up and feeders full, but this feels like a penetration of my home, an invasion. I live in the woods. Why build in my dormers? What's wrong with trees? It should be simple to get rid of them, although the pitch of the roof is steep and dangerous, but I can handle the logistics of the repair. The real problem is my granddaughters won't have it. How could I move the nests and restore the siding? "I'll move the nests to the branches of the shagbark hickory," I say. "What's wrong with that?" "What if the birds come back next year to find their home gone? Huh, Pa," Ellie will say. There's that word again. Pa. Pa would never snuff out life or destroy any creature's home; Pa loves all animals great and small; Pa marvels at baby racoons and fresh fawns. But Joe Mackall wants those fucking birds gone! What's a person to do? I used to know how to compartmentalize, but that survival skill has eluded me since becoming a grandfather. Championing the young is a charge hard to ignore.

I worry about my granddaughters living in a country and a world without my protection, even if I'm still around. I'm reminded of a time my son was about four. We were at my sister's house for a birthday party for a niece or nephew, and a bunch of the kids huddled at the top of the basement stairs. I knew somebody was going down. I didn't know until the next second that the child would be my son. The scene played out in slow motion as they so often do. I was two feet but somehow miles away, unable to reach him through the throng of young partiers, all cake-faced and safe. I watched as my son's head miraculously missed every single step. The miracle fall ended, however, when his head struck the concrete floor. While rushing down the stairs to hold him, I saw him look up to me with a Munch-like mouth wide open and still unable to scream or cry, with eyes that seemed to ask: 'Why didn't you, or couldn't you or wouldn't you save me?'

And that's how I feel most of the time as the grandfather of four granddaughters.

However, no matter how much I worry about the next generation I love, the dormer blackbirds must go. Perhaps this is the time to teach Ellie and Cassie the lesson that life's hard and you have to be harder. And yet I don't really believe that. Nor do I live that way. "They're only birds for the love of God," I want to scream, and that's true but it doesn't change a thing. I'll have to wage some kind of stealth operation to reclaim my home. I'll wait until the babies have flown the nest. Even Joe Mackall couldn't wall off mother and her chicks to die. The real issue is that my granddaughters love all new life, whatever it is. Even a blade of grass able to burst through tons of concrete in my driveway appears sacred. New life everywhere. Unstoppable life. But I'll have to tell my granddaughters what I did with the dormer birds. And it will have to be a good story, which means it will have to be true, which means there must be compassion for the lowly and a new sanctuary for the Jurassic squatters.

For now, sparrows chase away chickadees and cardinals scare blue jays and blue jays bend to the woodpeckers' will. And the black birds deliver worms all day long, in and out of my dormers like they're subletting the place. And my granddaughters cheer on the throng and pulse of existence. And I watch it all unfold, for the moment as Pa, falling under the spell that my home is a haven of safety, protecting me and my family from rain and hail and blizzards and other threats seen and unseen, a haven made of brick walls that might be able to stop a hail of bullets, but is easily permeated by the morning song of a single bird.

Yesterday's Noise

On a winter day in the early part of the 20th Century, my great-grandfather Casey walked carefully and quietly through the Pennsylvania woods. An avid hunter his entire life, on this day his quarry was deer. Not long into his hunt he saw something he'd never seen in his life. He froze, raised his rifle, pulled the trigger. The deer bounded briefly away, and then dropped. When my great-grandfather, still a young man on this day, spotted the deer again, he moved toward it until he felt that he could come no closer. He could do nothing but stare. What he observed at that moment was what had only seconds before been a perfect—and perfectly alive—albino doe. He then did what he'd always done: gutted it where it lay, skillfully tearing into its ivory hide with his hunting knife, leaving the entrails where they landed. When he'd finished dressing out his kill, the story goes, he could see nothing save patches of dark red blood on the deer and in the suddenly too white snow. The rest of it—sky and trees, ground and mountains, weapons and woods—fell away. Now all he witnessed was red death where there had been white life. He regretted the kill for the remainder of his days. For me the deer became a familial symbol. I believe on that day in the mountains of western Pennsylvania our genetic code shifted to accommodate the ugly truth that one of us had annihilated beauty.

Perhaps his kill nearly a century ago is the reason I'm becoming a believer in epigenetics, a theory espousing the idea that genes have memories and that the daily lives of our ancestors affect us today in myriad ways. Some psychologists even say we carry ancestral experiences within us, somewhere in our evolutionary subconscious. French psychologist Anne Ancelin Schutzenberger has written of what she calls the "ancestor syndrome." She believes we often have to acknowledge the suffering of our ancestors because we've been affected by it in our genetic memory. Just as our appearance and propensity for certain diseases have been passed down to us from ancestors we've never met, perhaps so too can experience, including suffering, for instance, and fear.

Some theorists on the fringe have gone so far as to suggest that if a person has an ostensibly irrational fear of wolves even while living in a fourth-floor walkup in New York City, the ancestor syndrome is at work. Perhaps a distant ancestor was attacked by a pack of wolves as she gathered raspberries from the back forty, while daydreaming about attending a dance in town later that night where she could show off her new calico dress.

Although the science is certainly dubious, I like believing it could be true. For the last few years, I've felt pulled by the past, as if long-dead ancestors are attempting to tell me something, to warn me of impending danger, to offer me lessons on the longevity and fragility of love. Perhaps this ancestral memory works the way stories of our childhood do. We swear we remember the experience of crawling out of our crib and turning on the television, because we've heard of it so often in family stories.

As long as I can remember, I've been a disciple and devotee of deer. I need to see them. I imagine them in deep woods and on the sides of hills. I search for sightings whenever I'm out, expecting to see deer eating in a field or drinking from a stream. I assume there's a lesson I'm supposed to learn from them. I call my wife the moment I spot one, as if I've just spied an ivory-billed woodpecker thought to be extinct. On the final day of the 20th Century, as the world prepared for the disaster that was to be Y2K, I felt secure in the passing of a century because that afternoon I had witnessed fourteen deer, two bucks and twelve does, walking through a field with a simple grace and a timeless endurance, doing what these animals have always done in the blue cold of a late December day.

Two other deer from the past haunt my psyche. My dad killed a buck while also hunting in western Pennsylvania. In a black and white photo, the only deer my dad ever killed lies roped to the hood of his two-year-old 1955 Chevy in a picture he'd sent to my mother just before they married. A few days before the kill, he'd sent my mom a postcard. It read, in full: "Hi, dear. No deer. Bye, dear." But in the photo an eight-point buck with a perfectly symmetrical rack covers the hood of the Chevy. For years the mounted head and upturned hooves hung in the basement of my childhood home. When I was a small boy, alone in our dank and dark basement, I feared the glass-eyed gaze of my father's trophy. I usually broke the spell of fear by rushing up the stairs screaming "I didn't kill you. You're dead and I'm not. You're dead and I'm not."

A few years ago, my father—who hasn't hunted in over four decades—was about to trash the mount because it had deteriorated so badly. Its ears hung loosely, ready to fall, and much of its fur appeared leprous. For no reason I can understand, I could not let him discard the deer that had been dead a year longer than I'd been alive. I needed to save it. I decided to take it to a taxidermist for repair, choosing one in western Pennsylvania, the place of the deer's death, although there are taxidermies near my rural Ohio home. When I was a kid and we'd visit the Pennsylvania relatives and landscape I loved, I knew we were closing in on our destination when we passed Kitzmiller's Taxidermy. I understood where I had to take the deer. I felt that to do it right, I must make the eight-hour round trip to have the mount repaired and a few months later, the eight-hour round trip to pick it up. When my wife asked why on earth I insisted on taking it to another state and spending two days driving, I could not give her a completely satisfactory answer. 'I'm pretty sure there's something wrong with me' was about the best explanation I could offer, which she seemed to accept. What I didn't tell her is that I talked to Buck (we were on a first-name basis before we'd reached the Pennsylvania line) most of the way there, at one point moving him to the front seat and affixing a baseball hat to his antlers, which I believe bestowed on me, on us really, the right to drive in the High Occupancy Vehicle lane.

The third deer that looms over me appeared in my life on the long-ago morning I walked out of my home and away from my first marriage, leaving my wife crying in the kitchen and my two-year-old son waving goodbye from behind the screen door. Sobbing to the point of actual stomach pain, I pulled onto the highway not a mile from the marriage and life I'd just pushed into the past, when I noticed a fawn, frightened and alone, clearly only a few weeks old, terrified and trapped between a forbidding fence and a dangerous highway. The symbolism of my son waving from behind the screen door and of the trapped fawn has haunted me for over thirty years, even though my ex-wife and I are friends and my son and I have a close and loving relationship. Still, and particularly when I'm with my son, his wife and their two tiny daughters, when laughter, love and joy pierce the skin of the day, this image of my son and the fawn creeps out of the mist of memory, and I feel the wound that comes with destroying a variant of beauty.

My ancestors not only hunted deer. They laid brick and made bread and delivered milk and mined coal. I'm obsessed with coal mines to the point of having dreams where I wake up with an aching back, squinting awake into shards of sun my window shades let in, as if it's the daylight my coal-mining paternal grandfather saw only on Sundays. I must also confess to a dumb love of mules, because my twelve-year-old grandfather's job was to lead the creatures into and out of the bowels of the mine. I want to own a mule or two just to have around my yard. I'd never make my mules work; I'd just let them hang, eat, drink, live life above ground. Some of my ancestors must have been ranchers, because I'd love to have a few longhorn steers, not to raise and harvest, but just to be able to look at through my kitchen window—and maybe to keep the mules company.

Why do I love an image of snow falling past gaslights on a street corner? The only reason I can think of stems from the story I heard about my maternal grandmother and her mother, standing beneath a streetlight reading a marriage license. My grandmother had been banished from the house because her abusive father hated that his Irish-light daughter married a dark-skinned Italian. Even though it pains me, I'm still enthralled by the image of these two women under a gaslight in the snow of a New York City night, the young girl exhilarated and anxious; her mother worried and maybe a little jealous, wondering if her daughter had discovered the love all the talk was about.

Lately I also have an unexplainable urge to begin canning fruits and vegetables the way my paternal grandmother did. I'm committed to making my own marmalade. On particular fall mornings I feel the itch to sew Halloween costumes for my granddaughters, the way my marmalade-making grandmother did for me. The cruel truth that I lack the skill to repair a hole in a sock does not deter me.

Sometimes I worry about my obsession with the past. It goes back as far as I can remember. The past seemed to me the place all story lived. Once upon a time that is not now. Then, not now. Stories of the past always had a beginning, middle and end. I don't recall when it happened, but I know it became a kind of felt truth that the past was more important, more meaningful, more lived, more narrative, more literary, more full of life and of what really mattered than the present could ever be, to say nothing of the future. The past was, somehow, more true.

As a child, my imagination seemed to jar loose and float back to the forties, the World War II years, known to me primarily through family stories (all of my maternal uncles had served in the war) as well as movies and music. Although my musical roots stretch deep and hard into rock 'n roll, I listened to music of the forties when I was alone, allowing myself to be seduced by melancholy, homesick for a time in which I'd never lived. On rainy afternoons alone in my room, I'd listen to the love songs of war and come to believe it was I who had fought in the French countryside, I who had made great war buddies from places like Enid, Oklahoma and Tupelo, Mississippi, I who mourned the girl I left at home who read my letters while sitting beneath a skinny sycamore tree. What got to me more than anything were the songs about lovers being apart. Could love survive war and distance? Could love outlive death? My adolescent sentimentality was fathomless. In my teens, the fifties took over. Too young to drive, my friends and I walked ten miles round trip to the dollar theater to see *American Graffiti* fifteen days in a row, always longing to live in a bygone age, loving the music, the romance, the restrained danger, the covert break from conformity. One night after returning from the movie, I broke from my friends and started a wild sprint through traffic-heavy Hauserman Road. As my friends looked on dumbfounded, I ran in and out of station wagons and pickup trucks, screaming nonsense, my head down, oblivious of brakes or horns or anything but my desire to see if I could trick my mind—or trick the mind of time—into permitting me access to 1950s America. Although this was certainly nearly all stunt and teenage exhibitionism, something happened that at first delighted and then scared the hell out of me. For a single moment on that crazed sprint it felt as if I had literally transcended the temporal. I no longer ran down a street in a suburb of Cleveland in 1973. I was, simply and somehow, elsewhere. I heard no cars or horns or cheers or laughs. I felt no night air on my skin. I had not run far enough or long enough to unleash endorphins. I simply became time mad, mad for the malleability or permeability of time. When I collapsed by the curb and felt the grass of my childhood summer, I looked around, surprised I was where I was, fully expecting to wake up in a counterclockwise world. My best friend said afterward that my face looked distorted; I became a friend he didn't recognize, a person he no longer knew. I often wonder if for that moment I'd slipped the temporal boundaries of the present, entered the relativity of time, if only viscerally, if only that once, as, perhaps, only an imaginative and puberty-pummeled kid can. I'm in love with what Charles Wright called "yesterday's noise." "How sweet the past is, no matter how wrong, or how sad," Wright wrote, "How sweet is yesterday's noise."

As I child I believed there were two kinds of people in the world. Those who—if time travel were possible—would propel themselves into the future, and those, like me, who would want to spiral into the past.

As of late I've been asking other questions. How much do we carry of those who have gone before us? How much do we pass on? What is our responsibility to those who are no longer here? What responsibility to live right and to remember well do we owe the children and grandchildren we leave behind?

Nearly a decade ago now, my brother and I attended our cousin's wedding, again in western Pennsylvania, so we stopped over to see our aunt who was too ailing to attend. I don't remember much of what we talked about that afternoon. Perhaps Aunt Mary fed us sugar cookies and cocoa. She's no longer around to ask. But I remember moment. As we were leaving her house that day, she said, "Now don't forget me." My brother and I assured her we would not. I can only guess why she said this. She had to have been in her late eighties then, and perhaps she could hear the train whistle in the distance growing louder—or fainter? I have no idea. I do know that I've not been able to forget her plea.

What I remember most about Aunt Mary was the way she consoled a grieving nine-year-old boy at his grandfather's funeral. I can recall her fingers running through my hair and down my wet cheeks. I have no idea what consoling words she offered, but I know she made me feel somehow better about the death of my grandfather, if only for a few minutes. Although I didn't know it at nine, Aunt Mary was an expert on death. When her daughter Annie was five years old, a dress she wore caught the flame of the gas stove as she passed by. Within minutes Annie was dead, burned to death because her pretty dress billowed into flame. Beauty annihilated.

Of course, I want to be alive and sensitive about what time and stories of the past are trying to teach me. And yet, I know above all things, that the present is where life ought to be lived. The certainty of this knowledge goes marrow deep. A few years ago, my wife and I had just returned from a trip to Utah's magnificent Monument Valley. We were still flush with the afterglow of a great vacation, on which we rode horses and let the rest of the world spin without us. But we hadn't seen our granddaughters in almost a week. Usually we can't go two or three days without a fix. When my oldest daughter brought the girls over that day, we burst out of the house to meet them in the driveway, racing to see who would reach them first. Soon we were doling our souvenirs and telling stories of our trip. Hugs and kisses everywhere. Little explosions of joy wherever we looked. We played with the girls at numerous toy stations in our house. When the two-year-old, Cassie, needed a nap, she went home, and Ellie, two years older, stayed "for a little while longer," as she always desires. She wanted to watch a movie and so we watched it together, she snuggling with us at any scene she found even mildly scary, even searching her shelves for a book to read, in case too many images were of dark rooms or dangerous storms. "I don't like twisters," she told us. And I know this as much as I know anything: that in these moments resides all of life. Love shared over an afternoon. Nothing glamorous or earth changing, just being with those we love and who love us. The stuff of an afternoon. The stuff of forever. But by tomorrow it will be yesterday, and lately, the rate at which the present produces the past overwhelms me.

The older I get the more the past seems poised to devour the present, pulling at me, wanting me to pay attention, demanding I tell certain stories, making sure I don't forget who and what have gone before, forcing me to keep the blood of my ancestors flowing. However, an ostensibly equal pull comes from my granddaughters, reminding me of the wonder of the present and the hope for the future. Separately and simultaneously these twin pulls of past and future hold me suspended over the present, as if over a river rimmed with rock canyons, the water beneath roiling with love and suffering, pain and joy.

I'd like to one day visit the mountain of my great-grandfather's ivory kill. I'd take my granddaughters with me. We'd climb through the snow and the hushed hills, and we'd search for an ever-elusive white deer. We might never see one, but we'd know, somehow, that it was out there. We'd descend the mountain on which we'd been elevated and surrounded by wonder, and then we'd go home, get warm, watch the steam rise from our hot chocolate, and tell the true and present story of all the beauty we'd encountered, all the beauty that survives.

Acknowledgements

Thanks to Steve Harvey, Bob Root and Kathy Winograd for the opportunity and for their friendship. To Dan Lehman for being my partner in *River Teeth: A Journal of Nonfiction Narrative* for the last twenty years. To Jill Christman, Mark Neely and the folks at Ball State University for joining *River Teeth* for the next twenty. To Russell Weaver, Tom Larson and Richard Hoffman for their friendship. Thanks to Andre Dubus III and Abigail Thomas, two of the best and most generous writers I know. And to Rick Holland for more than fifty years of being a damn fine old friend. To my dad, my siblings, my children and their spouses. To the memory of all my family who have come and gone. And to my wife, Dandi, without whom there would be nothing.

I'd also like to thank the editors and the publications in which earlier versions of some of these essays appeared: "The Private Wars of a Dying Storyteller," *The Cleveland Plain Dealer*; "Stories of the Working-Class Lights," *Writing Work*; "Words of My Youth," *Short Takes* (Norton); "The Teacher," *The Heartlands Today*; "The Little Girl at the Door," *Brevity*; "A Question of Laziness," *Chautauqua*; "Gazing at My Father Gazing," and "When You Write About Murder," *Solstice*; and "Yesterday's Noise," *Punctuate*.

Author's Study Guide: For Readers
Discussion Groups, Teachers, and Students

1. What does the author mean when he writes that he is "humbled" and "haunted" by history? He writes "I am not a prisoner of the past, but I am certainly caught up in it—by how today becomes yesterday." What are the distinctions between being a "prisoner of the past" and being "caught up" in it? Are there distinctions?

2. The author is not only obsessed with the past but also in the way the past becomes known, primarily through the stories told, by historians as well as family members. How has the author been molded by the stories of the past? How does he see his stories shaping the lives of his children and grandchildren?

3. How does the writer appear to reconcile (or not) his assertions about love in the passage "I understand that love is all we have, and I also realize how vulnerable love makes us"? Do you agree with the author's philosophy on the nature of love?

4. Discuss what you believe the author means when he writes, "I often feel as though I'm moving toward the edge of an emotional dystopia. I know it's connected in ways I don't fully understand to life as a grandfather...life as an American in a country increasingly polarized, fracked, outsourced, droned, downsized, teetering on the dream edge of itself." Do you share the writer's concerns about our country's future?

5. What aspects of the writer's character are revealed in "The Little Girl at the Door"? Does your opinion of him change from the beginning to the end of the piece? If so, how and why?

6. In "The Private Wars of a Dying Storyteller," the author describes his aging grandmother as achieving the perfect mix for storytelling, which he interprets as "memory, imagination and desire." How do these elements work for the nonfiction storyteller? How might they complicate a creative nonfiction writer's believability?

7. Discuss the last sentence in the essay "Words of My Youth." "The slur just seems to have been out there, there and somehow not there, like incense, like the way a Whiffle ball whips and dips, the way adults laugh at things kids don't understand, the way the background noise from a baseball game leaks out of transistor radios, the way factory fires flirt with the night sky, the way sonic booms burst the lie of silence."

8. Discuss why and how the author uses first-, second- and third-person points of view and past and present tense in "By Force, Threat, or Deception." Why does the author believe three points of view are necessary? Do you agree? Why does he shift between past and present tense? Are both imperative to the essay?

9. In the same essay the author writes competing versions of the night his uncle was murdered. Discuss why he does this. What does this say about the author's belief in the nature of storytelling?

Try to answer for yourself the following question the writer asks in "By Force, Threat, or Deception." "Does loving somebody and being a writer give you a right to his or her story?"

10. Discuss why the author includes the story of the killdeer in the essay "Gazing at My Father Gazing." How does the killdeer story reflect the concerns the writer has about the past, present and future in the more reflective sections of the essay? How does the story of the killdeer complement the themes of the essay?

11. The writer alludes to several historical figures in the book, most prominently Teddy Roosevelt, Abraham Lincoln, and John Brown. Why are these "stop-times" included in the collection? What do you see in these brief stories that are also discussed in other essays?

12. What does the writer mean by the sentence that appears at the opening of the essay "Yesterday's Noise"? He writes, "I believe on that day in the mountains of western Pennsylvania our genetic code shifted to accommodate the ugly truth that one of us had annihilated beauty." Discuss the Charles Wright poem the author uses as the epigraph for this book: *"How sweet the past is, no matter how wrong, or how/Sad./ How sweet is yesterday's noise."*

Made in the USA
Coppell, TX
19 November 2022

86653655R00090